Mary Shelley
in Bath

INTRODUCED BY
Fiona Sampson

Mary Shelley in Bath

MANDERLEY PRESS

Named for the house in Daphne du Maurier's novel *Rebecca*, Manderley Press finds forgotten or out-of-print books that were deeply inspired by a building, city or landmark, and brings those lost publications back to life for a contemporary audience.

We love selling our titles through bookshops around the world, and we especially delight in posting them to customers from our offices here in London. Ordering from us direct makes a huge difference to our independent press, allowing us to reinvest in future titles and exciting literary projects. As a thank you, we include matching bookmarks with each title, created exclusively for manderleypress.com readers.

The books all feature a specially commissioned introduction and cover, with both the author and the artist chosen for their connections to the places at the heart of each title. Cover artwork is also available to purchase, as signed giclée art prints.

Every Manderley Press title is exquisitely produced as a small hardback edition, printed on luxurious paper in the UK, and quarter-bound in real cloth with head and tail bands too.

For more information and a full list of published titles, please visit us at www.manderleypress.com

This hardback edition published in 2025 by Manderley Press
www.manderleypress.com

Introduction © Fiona Sampson 2025
Cover and illustrations © Eleanor Macnair 2025
With special thanks to Charles Robert Baker

All rights reserved. No part of this publication may be reproduced, stored in or introduced into a retrieval system, or transmitted, in any form, or by any means (electronic, mechanical, photocopying, recording or otherwise) without the prior written permission of the publisher.

ISBN: 978-1-0686613-0-3

Typeset in Chiswick and Chiswick Sans by Commercial Type
Designed by Myfanwy Vernon-Hunt, This-Side
Printed and bound by Gomer Press

CONTENTS

Introduction
Fiona Sampson
10

Publisher's Note
18

CHAPTER ONE
Mary Shelley's Journals
22

CHAPTER TWO
Mary Shelley's Letters
44

CHAPTER THREE
Frankenstein (Chapter 4)
58

CHAPTER FOUR

Short Stories

The Mourner

67

The Swiss Peasant

95

Transformation

123

The Mortal Immortal

147

Mary Shelley's Reading List in Bath

166

Suggested Further Reading

169

INTRODUCTION

Fiona Sampson

The Causes of a Life: Mary Shelley in Bath

Strictly speaking, of course, it wasn't Mary Shelley who arrived in Bath on 10 September 1816, but Mary Wollstonecraft Godwin. The nineteen-year-old who alighted in the city that Tuesday afternoon wasn't yet the wife of Percy Bysshe Shelley, the up-and-coming poet and heir to a baronetcy. Instead, she was his unmarried partner, as well as the mother of his third surviving child.

This was at the time an almost unthinkably radical arrangement, not least in Bath. Jane Austen's novels were at this very time examining the city's fashionable marriage market with delicate glee. But when Mary sat down to her late lunch that September day, 'free love' had already been framed as a revolutionary challenge to traditional institutions – the Church, the monarchy, marriage – by radical political philosophers, in particular the parents whose names she carried. Her mother, who died as a result of giving birth to her, had been Mary Wollstonecraft, author of *A Vindication of the Rights of Men* (1790) and *A Vindication of the*

Rights of Woman (1792). Wollstonecraft had married Mary's father, William Godwin, only after learning from experience with her own first child how hard it was to live as an unmarried mother at the end of the eighteenth century. Godwin, whose many disciples included Percy Bysshe Shelley, had also argued, in *Political Justice* (1793), for free love. But, by the time his daughter arrived in Bath that afternoon in early autumn, he had cut her off because of her unmarried relationship.

All the same, as she searched for lodgings that evening and again the next day, Mary was not alone. With her were her nine month-old, William, and his nursemaid Elise Duvillard. Little 'Wilmouse' was Mary's adored second child; her first-born had survived only a few days. But also in the party was her step-sister, Claire Clairmont, and it was for her sake they were in Bath. A few months Mary's junior and also unmarried, Claire was pregnant by Lord Byron; who was refusing to have anything to do with her. It was only a few months since the celebrated poet and peer, famously described by his former lover Lady Caroline Lamb as 'mad, bad and dangerous to know,' had been driven into exile by revelations in his divorce case. Claire's pregnancy was forcing the stepsisters to retreat from the gossipy centre of things in London. Where however Mary's own 'sweet elf' Percy was free to come and go, returning from time to time to her in Bath.

The writer we celebrate as Mary Shelley, pioneering woman and author of the first science fiction novel, *Frankenstein* (1818), as well as the first dystopian fiction, *The Last Man* (1826), lived from 1797 to 1851. But in all her life, the four months she was to spend in Bath would prove among the most important. For now, though, she was simply being a responsible sibling in a family crisis.

Claire had been a spoke in the wheel ever since Mary ran off with Percy at sixteen. On that whirlwind trip to Europe in 1814 – not an elopement, since the poet was already married, but something between a huge adventure and a sort of grooming – Claire had, bizarrely, come too. It had since proved impossible to displace her, not just from the household but from Percy's confidence. True, he had sent her away to Lynmouth in Devon for some eight months – conspicuously, long enough to have a baby. But she had since come roaring back into their lives and led them to the shores of Lake Geneva, where Byron was to spend the summer at Villa Diodati.

1816 would be remembered, however, as The Year Without a Summer. A huge volcanic eruption of Mount Tambora, in what was then the Dutch East Indies, had clouded earth's atmosphere with volcanic dust, causing wintry conditions in midsummer. Across northern Europe, peasant subsistence farmers were starving; just three days earlier, Mary's party had survived a rough Channel crossing on their way home from Geneva. Still, Claire had not lost her baby; and so here they were, marooned in Bath.

The accommodation Mary now found, at 5 Abbey Churchyard, was close to where they first arrived, in a district busy with the coaching inns so necessary for the resort's prosperity. The rooms were right in the centre of the social action: next door to the famous Pump Room, where invalids and holidaying socialites congregated to take the waters, see and be seen.

Appropriately enough, they were above 'Meyler's Circulating Library and Reading Rooms'. They also offered a glorious close-up of the Abbey's West Front, where angels clamber up and down Jacob's Ladder between heaven and earth: a proverb about aspiration and moral effort that could serve as a motto for Mary's *Frankenstein*. It was the perfect address for people watching and, had Mary but known it, for ghost hunting too, since the as yet un-rediscovered Roman Baths lay right beneath her feet.

And indeed, once she had settled Claire elsewhere, at 12 New Bond Street, she set to work on a ghost story. She was writing in response to a challenge. Three months earlier, in Geneva, Byron, his doctor John William Polidori, and Percy Bysshe had relieved the unseasonal gloom by discussing what Mary's Dr Frankenstein would call 'the causes of life.' Fresh-minted atheists, they wanted to reframe the Christian idea of a 'divine spark.' It was a fashionable topic. Experimental science, newly popular, was being disseminated by public lectures, including those Mary would attend at Bath's precursor to its Royal Literary and Scientific Institution in Queen Square. Twenty years earlier, the Italian scientific showman Luigi Galvani had appeared to demonstrate that biological life is electrical by publicly shocking the bodies of animals and executed criminals into motion; this belief was now being modified but his work, known as Galvanism, remained at the forefront of such discussions, including in Byron's salon.

A more recherché form of entertainment were German *Schauer-roman*, or shudder-stories, which went beyond stately British Gothick novels into necromancy and schlock. After the villa house party had read a collection of these, called *Phantasmagoriana*, Byron proposed they each write a ghost story. The game became something of a damp squib, like so much of that summer; both poets lost interest. But it sowed the seeds of both Polidori's 1819 short story *The Vampyre* and what would become Mary's second book.

At Abbey Churchyard, she started to devour fiction. For the previous couple of years, she had struggled through the classics to try and catch up with Percy's Eton and Oxford education. Now, probably taking advantage of the lending library downstairs, she read across the still-evolving novel genre, from *Gulliver's Travels* to *Don Quixote*, Richardson to Rousseau, and Walter Scott to Lady Caroline Lamb's recently published *roman à clef* about Byron, *Glenarvon*. She and Percy even read *Paradise Lost*, from which she would take the epigraph to *Frankenstein*.

We know this was research, not sheer book-wormery, because – as the pragmatic publisher's daughter she was – Mary would soon decide to enlarge her original 'ghost story' into a more saleable novel length, and cast around for a way to do so. Her triumphant formal solution was to nest three first person stories – the creature's, Frankenstein's and the Arctic explorer Captain Walton's – inside each other, making us match them up to each other. Mary didn't forget the science her fiction needed, either, whizzing through Humphrey Davy's *Introduction to Chemistry* at the end of October. She also took up drawing, with lessons on Mondays and Thursdays: although the curious journal entry for 8 October records having a Tuesday lesson instead.

Mary's journal entries were clipped to the point of code. The mysterious 'men dressed in black' accosting Percy on 20 October, for example, were debt collectors. As the daughter of famous, even notorious parents, she knew how much the written record could make or break a reputation; she was already writing for posterity. So on 8 October, she recorded simply, 'Letter from Fanny,' and, on 9 October, 'In the evening a very alarming letter comes from Fanny.'

But much is concealed here. 9 October was the very evening that Mary's 'other' sister, her half-sister Fanny Imlay, killed herself in a Swansea hotel. Mary Wollstonecraft's elder daughter had travelled alone – but *dressed in her mother's underwear* – from London to the embarkation port for Ireland. She was following in the footsteps of a pair of maternal aunts who first offered her a Dublin teaching post, then withdrew it because of her younger sister's sexual reputation.

'Our' Mary had a lot to feel responsible for, then. But why did she also use the journal to establish a (possibly false) alibi for 8 October; the day when Fanny had, as she told a fellow passenger, made an unnecessary coach change in Bath? Did Fanny – who had served as go-between for her sister and father, and may have been in love with Percy – come to see the couple, who were after all living so close by the town's coaching inns? Was she rebuffed? Fanny was often overlooked by her family, who regarded her as plain because she had her father's dark colouring. It's hard not to hear the echo of her sadness in Frankenstein's creature: 'I am alone and miserable. Only someone as ugly as I am could love me.'

Either way, suicide had now been added to the family quota of social shame. Yet Mary noted only '...the worst account. A miserable day. Two letters from Papa. Buy mourning...' Her letters were similarly rehearsed. On 5 December she wrote longingly to Percy, 'Give me a garden & absentia Clariae.' But neither the absence of Claire nor a garden were to come her way any time soon. Instead, on 15 December she recorded 'news of the death of Harriet Shelley.' Her lover's wife had drowned herself in the Serpentine lake in Hyde Park. Just twenty-one and heavily pregnant, Harriet had, like Mary, run away at sixteen with Percy despite his reputation. When she was abandoned, her family refused to take her back, leaving her with no means of support. Percy would always maintain the child she was carrying that December was not his, though it's hard for a modern reader to believe him. Willy-nilly, Mary wrote up the outcome with her habitual brevity. In London, 'A marriage takes place on the 30th December.'

Two deaths and a wedding, in a life-changing tangle. However much of a love match the new Mrs Shelley had made, hers was also a marriage of convenience, designed to prove to the Lord Chancellor that Percy was respectable enough to gain custody of his two children by Harriet. (In the event, he failed to do so.) The context was tragic, yet the marriage exciting: her child was now legitimate, and her father started speaking to her again. But, back in Bath, upheavals kept coming. On 12 January 1817, Claire gave birth to Byron's daughter, eventually to be named Allegra. In her journal Mary glossed over this, as well as her own part in helping out, as 'Four days of idleness.' Only on 24 January, when William turned one, did she feel able to note, with a rare burst of feeling: 'How many changes have occurred during this little year; may the ensuing one be more peaceful.' 'Nothing is so painful to the human mind as a great and sudden change,' as she would write in *Frankenstein*.

Two days after William's birthday, Mary was home in London. The strange, haunted passage in Bath was over. But she brought back with her the major part of what would become, when it was published anonymously on 1 January 1818, the book for which she is most remembered. And along with *Frankenstein* she brought the 'spark' of another life, too: for she was pregnant again. Clara would be born almost exactly a year after Mary Wollstonecraft Godwin arrived in Bath.

Fiona Sampson, 2025

PUBLISHER'S NOTE

Mary Shelley lived in Bath for a relatively short amount of time, but these few months represented a period of significant emotional and creative development, as an author, a mother, a friend, a sister, and eventually, as a wife as well. She stayed in the city at various times between 1816 and 1817, and during these visits, as detailed in Fiona Sampson's marvellous introduction to this book, she worked on multiple projects while also managing dark family secrets and experiencing several personal tragedies. It was here that her stepsister Claire Clairmont was confined to give birth to Lord Byron's illegitimate child; she would subsequently learn of the suicide of her half-sister, Fanny Imlay; and later, the death of her husband Percy Shelley's first wife, Harriet.

We have collected a selection of her work here in this book, not as an academic analysis of Mary Shelley's *oeuvre* (of which there are already many excellent examples: please see the Suggested Further Reading at the back of this book), but rather as a fascinating lens through which the reader can delve into Mary's world in Bath at this time.

Mary Shelley had begun to write her first novel – *Frankenstein; or, The Modern Prometheus* – while staying at the Villa Diodati near Lake Geneva, Switzerland in 1816. By the time she returned to England and had taken residence in Bath later that year, she was deeply engrossed in writing and refining the manuscript, which she completed in May 1817. Chapter Four of *Frankenstein* was written in her lodgings in 5 Abbey Churchyard – in the shadow of Bath's gothic abbey – and she notes this completion in her letter to Shelley (see p.45).

Though Bath itself does not appear as a direct setting in *Frankenstein*, its societal influences, as well as the intellectual circles Mary moved in, no doubt influenced the novel's gothic and existential themes. Mary's own feelings of being disconnected from high society, and of observing it from the fringes in Bath, may also have subtly influenced the social dynamics and class themes that appear in her later works, especially the isolation felt by Frankenstein's creature – the archetypal outcast.

During this time, Mary also wrote numerous journal entries and letters, and we have included a selection of these in Chapters One and Two. They provide valuable insights into her personal life, her thoughts on her work, as well as her interactions with friends and family. The letters from this period often reflect her struggles with grief as well as the social and financial difficulties she faced.

While *Frankenstein* was the most significant of Mary's work written in Bath, we have also chosen several short stories to include in this collection that can be linked to her life during this period. They were written some time after Mary had left the city, and none of them were explicitly set there, but they may well have been influenced by the emotional and social landscape she experienced during these months. Mary's works from this period reflect an evolving literary style and a focus on gothic and melancholic themes.

Some of these themes can be identified in the stories we have chosen below: 'The Mourner', for example, written in 1829, is a short story dealing with loss and mourning, and although completed later in life (following the deaths of three of her four children and her husband), the seeds were certainly planted during earlier years, including Mary's time in Bath; 'The Swiss Peasant' (1830) is another of Mary's short stories that delves into social issues and personal relationships, and aligns with her broader interests in the human condition and societal structures; 'Transformation' – published in 1831 – features a blend of gothic revenge and supernatural elements, exploring themes of identity and human nature and reflecting on the darker aspects of Mary's writing style that were honed during her formative years, including most probably, her stay in Bath; while 'The Mortal Immortal', from 1833, looks at themes of immortality and the human condition, and also showcases the gothic elements and philosophical enquiries that Mary Shelley became associated with as an author.

Bath was known for its libraries, bookshops, assemblies, lectures, and social gatherings, which drew a diverse group of people. The Pump Room, the Assembly Rooms and the Kingston Lecture Room were popular venues for intellectual and cultural gatherings, attracting philosophers, writers and scientists who shared and discussed new ideas. Mary's engagement with these lectures highlights her keen interest in science and philosophy.

This fascination would profoundly shape her work, particularly in her portrayal of the character Victor Frankenstein, whose obsession with understanding and harnessing the secrets of life drives the narrative of her novel.

Mary was exposed to a variety of scientific and philosophical ideas shared through public lectures, local physicians, visiting scholars and the intellectual circles she was part of while living in Bath. Topics of discussion included electricity and Galvanism, chemistry and biology and a general philosophy of science. Emerging ideas about the chemical processes of life, early understandings of biology, as well as debates on the ethical implications and the philosophical questions surrounding the pursuit of scientific knowledge, were critical to the themes in *Frankenstein* and Mary's later short stories too.

Bath's cultural and intellectual environment provided the perfect backdrop to Mary's evolution as an author. Her time there was therefore undeniably formative: Bath provided Mary with a space to reflect, grieve and write, all of which fed into her literary output, and her legacy as the author of the first science-fiction novel, and one of the most important figures in English literature.

Rebeka Russell, 2025

CHAPTER ONE

Mary Shelley's Journals

Monday, September 9

We are kept here until 2 o'clock by the Custom-house. Take leave of Shelley, and go as far as Salisbury, on our way to Bath. [Shelley went to London.]

Tuesday, September 10

Arrive at Bath about 2. Dine, and spend the evening in looking for lodgings. Read Mrs. Robinson's *Valcenza*.

Wednesday, September 11

Look for lodgings; take some, and settle ourselves. Read the 1st vol. of *The Antiquity* [by Scott], and work. [Lodgings were found at 5 Abbey Church Yard, Bath.]

Thursday, September 12

Letter from Shelley. Read the *Edinburgh Review* and the 2nd volume of *The Antiquary*.

Friday, September 13
Letter from Shelley; write to him. Read *Chrononhotonthologus* [a burlesque drama by Henry Carey, 1734], put things away, and work.

Saturday, September 14
Read *Fazio, Love and Madness* [by the Reverend Sir Herbert Croft, 1780], and some of *Rienzi*; work; in the evening finish *The Antiquary*.

Sunday, September 15
Read *Rienzi*; in the evening walk out; read the *Solitary Wanderer* [by Charlotte Smith, 1800]. Letter from Shelley; he is with Peacock [Thomas L. Peacock, 1785–1866, was an English novelist, poet and official of the East India Company. He met Shelley in 1812 and remained his life-long devoted friend and travelling companion].

Monday, September 16
Write, and read the *Memoirs of the Princess of Bareith*; work; Shelley is searching for a house about Marlow.

Tuesday, September 17
Read the *Memoirs* aloud; write to Shelley.

Wednesday, September 18
Read the *Memoirs*. A letter from Shelley. Write.

Thursday, September 19

Set out from Bath; travel until 4 o'clock, when I arrive at Maidenhead. Shelley and Peacock are there to meet me. We walk to Marlow. In the evening read the Letters of *Emile* [by Rousseau].

Friday, September 20

Walk to the Fisherman's Cliff and Medmenham Abbey; return about 4. Finish the Letters of *Emile*, and read a part of *Clarissa Harlowe* [Richardson's *Clarissa*].

Saturday, September 21

Shelley and Peacock walk out. Read vol. 6 of *Clarissa*.

Sunday, September 22

Peacock and Shelley walk out. Read vol. 7 of *Clarissa*. Shelley reads the Letters of *Emile*.

Monday, September 23

Read volume 8 of *Clarissa*. Shelley and Peacock walk out. I take a short walk with Mrs. P[eacock]. Peacock's Uncle comes in the evening.

Tuesday, September 24

Shelley goes up to London. Read [Johnson's] *The Rambler*. Shelley reads Montaigne's *Essays*. He does not return until 11 o'clock.

Wednesday, September 25

Return to Bath with Shelley; we arrive between 8 and 9, and talk of our plans the rest of the evening.

Thursday, September 26

Shelley and I walk out in the morning and evening; talk of our plans; work.

Friday, September 27

Read *Curtius*, and work. Read the *Memoirs of the Princess of Bareith* aloud in the evening; walk.

Saturday, September 28

Work, and read the *Memoirs* in the evening; walk with Shelley for two or three hours; work. Shelley reads Peter Pindar's [John Wolcot's] book aloud.

Sunday, September 29

Read Clarendon [*History of the Rebellion and Civil Wars in England*] all day. Shelley writes to Albe [Byron], and other things, he finishes Lacretelle's *History of the French Revolution*. We walk out for a short time after dinner. Shelley reads Lucian.

Monday, September 30

Shelley spends the day at Bristol. Read the *Memoirs* aloud, and begin the *Life of Holcroft*.

Tuesday, October 1

Shelley reads the *Life of Holcroft* aloud all day. Read the *Memoirs of the Princess of Bareith*.

Wednesday, October 2

Read Clarendon; finish the *Life of Holcroft*; read [Lady C. Lamb's] *Glenarvon* in the evening; write to Fanny.

Thursday, October 3

Not well. Read *Glenarvon* all day, and finish it.

Friday, October 4

Read *Clarendon*; walk out with Shelley; and get letter from Fanny.

Saturday, October 5

Read Clarendon and Curtius; walk with Shelley. Shelley reads Tasso.

Sunday, October 6

[*Shelley*] On this day Mary put her head through the door and said, 'Come and look; here's a cat eating roses; she'll turn into a woman; when beasts eat these roses they turn into men and women.'

[*Mary*] Read Clarendon all day; finish the 11th book. Shelley reads Tasso.

Monday, October 7

Read Curtius and Clarendon; write. Shelley reads *Don Quixote* aloud in the evening.

Tuesday, October 8

Letter from Fanny [written at Bristol]. Drawing lesson. Walk out with Shelley to the South Parade, read Clarendon, and draw. In the evening work, and Shelley reads *Don Quixote*; afterwards read *Memoirs of the Princess of Bareith* aloud.

Wednesday, October 9

Read Curtius; finish the *Memoirs of the Princess of Bareith*; draw. In the evening a very alarming letter comes from Fanny. Shelley goes immediately to Bristol; we sit up for him till 2 in the morning, when he returns, but brings no particular news. [Fanny committed suicide on the night of October 9.]

Thursday, October 10

Shelley goes again to Bristol, and obtains more certain trace. Work and read. He returns at 11 o'clock.

Friday, October 11

He sets off to Swansea. Work and read.

Saturday, October 12

He returns with the worst account. A miserable day. Two letters from Papa. Buy mourning, and work in the evening.

Sunday, October 13

Read *Patronage* [by Maria Edgeworth] and the *Milesian Chief* [a novel by Charles Robert Maturin]; finish 5th volume of Clarendon. Shelley reads *Life of Cromwell.*

Monday, October 14

Finish *Milesian* and *Patronage*; read *Holcroft's Travels*. [Thomas Holcroft, *Travels from Hamburg through Westphalia, Holland, and the Netherlands*, 1804] Shelley reads *Life of Cromwell.*

Tuesday, October 15

Read Clarendon, draw, walk, and work. Letter from Papa.

Wednesday, October 16

Read Clarendon, draw, and walk.

Thursday, October 17

Drawing lesson. Read *Alphonsine* [by Madame de Genlis, 1807]. Shelley reads *Don Quixote* aloud. Walk; read Latin.

Friday, October 18

Shelley reads Montaigne. Read Clarendon, walk, write.

Saturday, October 19

Work; write. Shelley reads Montaigne. Read Clarendon. In the evening, Shelley reads *Don Quixote* aloud.

Sunday, October 20

Write. Shelley attempts going to Oxford, but is stopped by the men dressed in black; he leaves them, however, and returns home. He reads Montaigne. Read Clarendon and *O'Donnel*.

Monday, October 21

Drawing lesson. Clare and Shelley walk out. Read Clarendon, and draw and write. Shelley reads Montaigne and Lucian; reads *Don Quixote* aloud.

Tuesday, October 22

Draw and write; read Clarendon, and finish the 14th book; work in the evening, and read Curtius. Shelley writes, and reads Montaigne and Lucian, and walks.

Wednesday, October 23

Walk before breakfast; afterwards write, and read Clarendon. Shelley writes, and reads Montaigne. In the evening read Curtius, and work. Shelley reads *Don Quixote* aloud.

Thursday, October 24

Drawing lesson. Read Clarendon; write; after dinner read Curtius. Shelley reads Montaigne; after tea, he reads *Don Quixote* aloud.

Friday, October 25

Draw, write, and read Clarendon. Shelley reads Montaigne. Read Curtius. After tea Shelley reads *Don Quixote* aloud.

Saturday, October 26

[Shelley] Mary writes her book, and reads Clarendon. Description of a Cave, in the *Morning Chronicle*. Shelley from this day determines to keep an account of how much food he eats; consumes in the day 22 ounces. Shelley reads Montaigne; writes; walks.

Sunday, October 27

[*Shelley*] B. 3.07, 12 gr. L. 3 oz. Write Ch. $2\frac{1}{2}$ [these entries are Percy's calculations of how much he has eaten on those days]. [*Mary*] Finish Clarendon's *History*. Shelley reads Montaigne. [*Shelley*] D. 1307. T. 4.07, 4.9. In all 3.0712 gr. L. 307. D. 1.307. T. 407.45–24.07.
[*Mary*] Read Curtius and *Rienzi*. Shelley reads *Don Quixote* aloud.

Monday, October 28.

[*Mary*] A drawing lesson. Read the Introduction to Sir H. Davy's *Chemistry*, write; in the evening read Anson's *Voyages* [George, Baron Anson, *A Voyage Round the World*, 1748] and Curtius. Shelley reads *Don Quixote* aloud after tea. Finish Anson's *Voyages* before night.

Tuesday, October 29

Draw; read Davy's *Chemistry* with Shelley; read Curtius and Ide's *Travels*. Shelley reads Montaigne, and *Don Quixote* aloud in the evening.

Wednesday, October 30

Read Davy's *Chemistry*. Letters from Charles. Draw, and write to him. Read Ide's *Travels* and Curtius in the evening. Shelley reads Montaigne, and *Don Quixote* aloud in the evening.

Thursday, October 31

Drawing lesson. Afterwards Shelley is called for by Mr. Lawes; talk with him. Read Ide's *Travels*. Shelley reads *Don Quixote* aloud in the evening.

Friday, November 1

Shelley is teased all the day by Mr. Lawes. Draw, and read *Don Quixote* in the evening.

Saturday, November 2

Shelley calls at the Greyhound. Write; read Davy. In the evening read Curtius and *Les Incas* [by Jean François Marmontel, 1777] and work. Shelley writes a little, and reads Montaigne. Draw.

Sunday, November 3

Draw, write; read *Les Incas*. Shelley reads Montaigne; walks. In the evening read Curtius, and Shelley reads *Don Quixote* aloud.

Monday, November 4

Draw, write; read Davy; in the evening Curtius and *Don Quixote*. Shelley reads Montaigne.

Tuesday, November 5

Draw, and read *Bryan Perdue*. Shelley reads Montaigne and *Don Quixote*. Work in the evening.

Wednesday, November 6

Draw; finish *Bryan Perdue*; write. Not well in the evening. Begin *Sir C. Grandison*. [Richardson, *The History of Sir Charles Grandison*.]

Thursday, November 7

Drawing lesson. Walk; read *Sir C. Grandison*. Shelley reads Montaigne in the morning, and finishes *Don Quixote* in the evening.

Friday, November 8

Draw, walk, and read *Sir C. Grandison*. Shelley reads Montaigne. Read Curtius, and [Maria Edgeworth's] *Castle Rackrent* aloud. I finish *Castle Rackrent* in the evening.

Saturday, November 9

Write; read *Grandison*; read Curtius. Shelley reads *Gulliver's Travels* aloud, and Montaigne in the morning.

Sunday, November 10

Draw; read *Grandison* and Curtius. Shelley reads and finishes Montaigne, to his great sorrow. He reads Lucian.

Monday, November 11

Drawing lesson. Read *Grandison*, write, and read Curtius. Shelley reads Lucian and *Gulliver's Travels* in the evening.

Tuesday, November 12

Walk, and read *Grandison* and Curtius; work in the evening. Shelley reads Lucian, and goes to bed early.

Wednesday, November 13

Read *Grandison*; write. Shelley reads Lucian and *Gulliver* in the evening. Work; walk.

Thursday, November 14

Read *Grandison*. Drawing lesson. Walk; read Curtius. Shelley reads Lucian. After tea, work. Shelley reads *Gulliver* aloud.

Friday, November 15

Write; finish *Grandison*; walk. Shelley reads Locke. Read Curtius after dinner; after tea work. Shelley finishes *Gulliver*, and begins *Paradise Lost*.

Saturday, November 16

Draw, write; read old voyages; not well; read Curtius. In the evening Shelley reads 2nd book of *Paradise Lost*. Shelley reads Locke.

Sunday, November 17

Draw, write; read Locke and Curtius. Shelley reads Plutarch and Locke; he reads *Paradise Lost* aloud in the evening, I work.

Monday, November 18

Drawing lesson. Write, and read Locke. Shelley walks with Clare; reads Locke and Plutarch. Read Curtius; work in the evening. Shelley reads *Paradise Lost* aloud.

Tuesday, November 19

Walk to the higher Crescent to see the Eclipse, but is too cloudy; see many disconsolate people with burnt glass. Finish 1st book of Locke, read Curtius, and work. Shelley reads Locke, Plutarch, and *Paradise Lost* aloud. Letter from Albe.

Wednesday, November 20

Draw and write; read Locke and Curtius; begin [Richardson's] *Pamela*. Shelley reads Locke, and in the evening *Paradise Lost* aloud to me.

Thursday, November 21

Drawing lesson. Write, read Locke, and walk out; after dinner read Curtius. After tea Shelley reads *Paradise Lost* aloud. Read *Pamela*. Little Babe not well. Shelley reads Locke and *Pamela*.

Friday, November 22

Draw, read Locke, and write; walk after dinner; read Curtius.

Shelley reads Locke and Curtius, and finishes *Paradise Lost*;
reads *Pamela* aloud.

Saturday, November 23
Babe is not well. Write, draw and walk; read Locke. Shelley
reads Locke and Curtius, and *Pamela* aloud in the evening.
Elise goes to the play. [Elise was a Swiss nurse who travelled
with with Mary and Percy from Geneva. She remained in their
service until early 1819, leaving them at Naples after marrying.]

Sunday, November 24
Write, read Locke, and draw; walk after dinner; read Curtius
and *Pamela*; work. After tea Shelley reads Curtius.

Monday, November 25
Write, and read Locke; draw, and walk. Shelley reads Curtius
and Plutarch. Read *Pamela*, and Shelley reads Gibbon, after tea.

Tuesday, November 26
Write, draw, and read Locke. Shelley reads Plutarch. Walk; read
Pamela, after, read Curtius and *Les Incas* Shelley reads Gibbon
in the evening; goes out to take a little walk, and loses himself.

Wednesday, November 27
Write; read Locke and *Pamela*; Curtius after tea. Shelley is
not well; he reads Plutarch. Work in the evening, and read
Les Incas.

Thursday, November 28
Drawing lesson. Write; read *Pamela*; in the evening I finish Curtius. Shelley reads and finishes Plutarch's *Life of Alexander*. After tea, Shelley reads the 20th chapter of Gibbon to me.

Friday, November 29
Write, read Locke, and walk; after dinner, read some of Livy, but am stopped by the badness of the edition. Shelley reads *Political Justice* and the 21st chapter of Gibbon aloud. Read *Pamela*.

Saturday, November 30
Finish *Pamela*; draw, write, read Locke, and walk. Shelley reads *Political Justice* and 22nd chapter of Gibbon. Read two Odes of Horace.

Sunday, December 1
Letter from Leigh Hunt. Send the present of Mathews. Write; read Locke, and the *Edinburgh Review*, and two Odes of Horace. Shelley reads *Political Justice* and Shakespeare, and the 23rd chapter of Gibbon.

Monday, December 2
Drawing lesson. Write, read Locke, and walk. Shelley reads Roscoe's *Life of Lorenzo de Medicis*. Read Lucian, and work in the evening; read several Odes of Horace.

Tuesday, December 3

Write; draw; read Locke and the *Life of Lorenzo*. Shelley reads it, and finishes it. In the evening he reads 25th chapter of Gibbon and several Odes of Horace.

Wednesday, December 4

A letter from Mrs. Godwin to Clare, and to me a letter from Aunt Everina concerning my sister [Fanny]. Write; read the *Life of Lorenzo*. Shelley reads the Appendix, and writes to Hayward and Papa; he reads the 25th chapter of Gibbon aloud.

Thursday, December 5

Shelley sets off for Marlow. Drawing lesson. Write; send a letter to Aunt Everina [and a letter to] Shelley [see p.44]. Read Lucian aloud to Clare; one Ode of Horace; in the evening, the *Quarterly Review* and Locke.

Friday, December 6

Read Lucian; write; draw; read Horace. Letter from Mrs. Godwin and 100*l*. Write to Mrs. Godwin and Shelley; work; read the *Rights of Women* [by her mother, Mary Wollstonecraft].

Saturday, December 7

Walk; write; read the *Rights of Women*; *Opuscula* of Cicero; read Lucian, and work; draw.

Mary Shelley in Bath 37

Sunday, December 8

Write; read *Rights of Women*; *Opuscula*.

Monday, December 9

Drawing lesson. Letters from Mrs. Godwin and Charles Clairmont. Write; finish the *Rights of Women*; begin Chesterfield's *Letters to his Son*; read *Opuscula*; work.

Tuesday, December 10

Write; read Locke and Chesterfield, 'De Senectute', and *The Wanderer*. [A long poem by Richard Savage, 1729.]

Wednesday, December 11

Draw; write; read *The Wanderer*; read 'De Senectute' and Chesterfield.

Thursday, December 12

Letter from Shelley; he has gone to visit Leigh Hunt. A letter from Leigh Hunt. Drawing lesson. Read Chesterfield, Locke, and 'De Senectute'.

Friday, December 13

Write; read Locke, 'De Senectute', and Chesterfield; draw. Letter from Shelley; he is pleased with Hunt.

Saturday, December 14

Draw; finish 'Senectute'; read Chesterfield.

Saturday, December 14 (cont.)

Shelley comes back in the evening.

Sunday, December 15

Draw. A letter from [Thomas] Hookham with the news of the death of Harriet Shelley. Walk out with Shelley. He goes to town after dinner. Read Chesterfield. [Harriet's body had been found in the Serpentine on December 10.]

Monday, December 16[-31]

I have omitted writing my Journal for some time. Shelley goes to London and returns; I go with him; spend the time between Leigh Hunt's and Godwin's. A marriage takes place on the 30th of December, 1816. Draw; read Lord Chesterfield and Locke. [Shelley and Mary were married at St. Mildred's Church, London, on December 30, 1816]

1817

Wednesday, Jan. 1

Return from London; travel all day; unwell.

Thursday, Jan. 2.

Read Lord Chesterfield's *Letters*; part of the *Lay Sermon* [by Coleridge]. Shelley writes.

Friday, Jan. 3

Read Lord Chesterfield; write; finish the *Lay Sermon*. Shelley writes.

Saturday, Jan. 4

Read Lord Chesterfield; write; work. Shelley writes.

Sunday, Jan. 5

Finish Lord Chesterfield; read *Douglas* [probably the tragedy by John Home] and *The Gamester*; write. Shelley writes.

Monday, Jan. 6

Shelley goes to London. Write; read several papers in [Addison's] *The Spectator*, Locke, and *Memoirs of Count Gramont* [by Anthony Hamilton]. Meeting held here; very quiet.

Tuesday, Jan. 7

Write; read *Life of Clarendon* [by Edward Hyde, Earl of Clarendon, 1759]; walk; read a little Latin; work.

Wednesday, Jan. 8

Write; read Locke; walk; read *Life of Clarendon*; work.

Thursday, Jan. 9

Walk out all the morning; read [Cicero's] *Somnium Scipionis* and [Smollett's] *Roderick Random*.

Friday, Jan. 10
Write; finish *Roderick Random*; work.

Saturday, Jan. 11
–

Sunday, Jan. 12 [11–15]
C. C. [may refer to a letter from Charles Clairmont, who was in France]. Four days of idleness. Letters from Shelley; he is obliged to stay in London. Read *Comus*; *Knights of the Swan* [by Madame de Genlis]; 1st volume of Goldsmith's *Citizen of the World*.

* Claire's baby Alba (renamed Allegra in 1818) was born on 12 January, which explains why Mary described the neglect of her journal as 'idleness'. From *Mary Shelley's Journal* (Frederick L. Jones (ed.), 1947): 'Mary's reticence concerning Claire, especially her connection with Byron, is emphatically indicated by her failure to record the birth of Claire's child, which she even hides from prying eyes under "Four days of idleness." In fact, Mary is very cautious about recording any personal matters.'

Thursday, Jan. 16
Read [Richard] Cumberland's *Memoirs*; work.

Friday, Jan. 17
Read *Memoirs*; walk out, and work.

Saturday, Jan. 18

Read *Memoirs*, and work.

Sunday, Jan. 19

Finish the *Memoirs* of Cumberland; read [Johnson's] *The Rambler*.

Monday, Jan. 20

Read Junius. Rain all day. Work.

Tuesday, Jan. 21

Walk out, work, and read [Letters of] Junius; read *Amadis*. [Vasco de Lobeira, Amadis de Gaul, trans. by Robert Southey.]

Wednesday, Jan. 22

Read Junius, *Somnium Scipionis*, and work; read *Amadis of Gaul*.

Thursday, Jan. 23

Read and finish Junius; finish *Somnium Scipionis*; work; read *Amadis*.

Friday, Jan. 24

My William's birthday. How many changes have occurred during this little year; may the ensuing one be more peaceful, and my William's star be a fortunate one to rule the decision of this day.* Alas! I fear it will be put off, and the influence of the star pass away. Read the [*The Countess of Pembroke's*] *Arcadia* [by Sir Philip Sidney] and *Amadis*; walk with my sweet babe.

* This is a reference to the Chancery proceedings concerning Shelley's children by Harriet.

Saturday, Jan. 25
An unhappy day. I receive bad news, and determine to go up to London. Read the *Arcadia* and *Amadis*. Letter from Mrs. Godwin and William [Godwin, Jr.].

Sunday, Jan. 26
Journey to town. Mrs. Godwin and William at the inn to meet me.

CHAPTER TWO

Mary Shelley's Letters

TO PERCY SHELLEY

Bath, New Bond Street
December 5th 1816

Sweet Elf

I got up very late this morning so that I could not attend Mr West. I dont know any more. Good night.

[John West (1772-1836), was a miniature painter and a drawing master, who gave weekly lessons to Mary in Bath.]

TO PERCY SHELLEY

December 5th, 1816
Bath

Sweet Elf

I was awakened this morning by my pretty babe and was dressed time enough to take my lesson from Mr West and (Thank God) finished that tedious ugly picture I have been so long about – I have also finished the 4 Chap. of Frankenstein which is a very long one & I think you would like it.

And where are you? and what are you doing my blessed love; I hope and trust that for my sake you did not go outside this wretched day, while the wind howls and the clouds seem to threaten rain. And what did my love think of as he rode along – Did he think about our home, our babe and his poor Pecksie? But I am sure you did and thought of them all with joy and hope. – But in the choice of residence dear Shelley pray be not too quick or atatch [*sic.*] yourself too much to one spot – Ah – were you indeed a winged Elf and could soar over mountains & seas and could pounce on the little spot – A house with a lawn a river or lake – noble trees & divine mountains that should be our little mousehole to retire to – But never mind this – give me a garden & absentia Clariæ and I will thank my love for many favours.

If you, my love, go to London you will perhaps try to procure a good Livy, for I wish very much to read it – I must be more industrious especially in learning latin which I neglected shamefully last summer at intervals, and those periods of not reading at all put me back very far.

The morning Chronicle[1] as you will see does not make much of the riots which they say are entirely quieted and you would almost be enclined to say out of the mountain comes forth a mouse [Horace, *Ars Poetica*, line 139] although I dare say poor Mrs Platt does not think so

The blue eyes of your sweet boy are staring at me while I write this he is a dear child and you love him tenderly, although I fancy your affection will encrease when he has a nursery to himself and only comes to you just dressed and in good humour – Besides when that comes to pass he will be a wise little man for he improves in mind rapidly – Tell me shall you be happy to have another little squaller? You will look grave on this, but I do not mean anything.

Leigh Hunt[2] has not written; – I would advise [a] letter addressed to him at the Examiner office if there is no answer tomorrow – he may not be at the vale of Health for it is odd that he does not acknowledge the receipt of so large a sum. There have been no letters of any kind today.

Now, my dear, when shall I see you? Do not be very long away! Take care of yourself; & take a house. I have a great fear that bad weather will set in. My airy Elf, how unlucky you are! I shall write to Mrs G. [Godwin] but let me know what you hear from Hayward and Papa as I am greatly interrested in those affairs.[3] Adieu, sweetest, Love me tenderly and think of me with affection whenever any thing pleases you greatly

Your affectionate girl
Mary W.G.

[*P. S., sideways*] I have not asked Clare but I dare say she would send her love although I dare say she would scold you well if you were here. My compts & remembrances to Dame Peacock & son – but [do] not let them see this – sweet, adieu

ADDRESS: Percy B. Shelley Esq / Great Marlow / Bucks.
POSTMARK: [BA]TH / [DEC.] 5 / [18]16.

Background Notes

After returning to England on 8 September, Shelley went to London on business and then to Marlow to find a house, while Mary Godwin and Claire Clairmont travelled straight to Bath. This plan was devised to prevent the Godwins from discovering that Claire Clairmont was expecting Byron's child.

[1] On 4 December, it was reported in the *Morning Chronicle* that on 2 December, rioters intended to collect arms and journey to Carlton House, home of the Prince Regent. Mr. Platt, a neighbour of Godwin's, living on Skinner Street, was wounded by those rioters demanding firearms.

[2] James Henry Leigh Hunt (1784-1859), was a poet, essayist, editor and co-owner of a weekly newspaper, the *Examiner*. Percy Shelley admired Hunt's liberal views and had written to him on several times, even offering him money (which he in turn declined) after he was jailed for libelling the Prince Regent. Hunt's article 'Young Poets' (regarding the work of Keats, Shelley, and Reynolds), which appeared in the *Examiner* on 1 December, resulted in a firm friendship between the two men. Mary's letter of 5 December suggests Shelley had once again sent funds to Hunt.

[3] These 'affairs' may refer to Fanny Imlay's letter of 3 October, in which she reminded Mary of various financial promises that Shelley had made to her father.

TO PERCY SHELLEY

Bath
December 17th, 1816

My beloved friend

I waited with the greatest anxiety for your letter – You are well & that assurance has restored some peace to me.

How very happy shall I be to possess those darling treasures that are yours – I do not exactly understand what Chancery has to do in this and wait with impatience for tomorrow when I shall hear whether they are with you and then what will you do with them? My heart says bring them instantly here – but I submit to your prudence

You do not mention Godwin – When I receive your letter tomorrow I shall write to Mrs G. [Godwin] I hope yet I fear that he will show on this occasion some disinterrestedness – Poor dear Fanny if she had lived until this moment she would have been saved for my house would then have been a proper assylum for her[1] – Ah! my best love to you do I owe every joy every perfection that I may enjoy or boast of – Love me, sweet, for ever – But I [do] not mean ---- I hardly know what I mean I am so much agitated

Clare has a very bad cough but I think she is better today Mr Cam [a surgeon, living at 7 Alfred Street, Bath] talks of bleeding if she does not recover quickly – but [she] is positively resolved not to submit to that – She sends her love

My sweet love deliver some message from me to your kind friends at Ham[p]stead – Tell Mrs Hunt that I am extremely obliged to her for the little profile she was so kind as to send me[2] and thank Mr H. [Hunt] for his friendly message which I did not hear

These Westbrooks – But they have nothing to do with your sweet babes they are yours and I do not see the pretence for a suit but tomorrow I shall know all

Your box arrived today I shall send soon to the upholsterer – for now I long more than ever that our house should be quickly ready for the reception of those dear children whom I love so tenderly then there will be a sweet brother and sister for my William who will lose his pre-eminence as eldest and be helped third at table – as his Aunt Clare is continually reminding him–

Come down to me sweetest as soon as you can for I long to see you and embrace – As to the event you allude [to] be governed by your friends & prudence as to when it ought to take place but it must be in London[3]

Clare has just looked in – she begs you not to stay away long – to be more explicit in your letters and sends her love

You tell me to write a long letter and I would but that my ideas wander and my hand trembles come back to reassure me my Shelley & bring with you Your darling Ianthe & Charles – Thank your kind friends I long to hear about Godwin

Your Affectionate Companion
Mary – W.G. –

Have you called on Hogg [4] I would hardly advise you – Remember me sweet in your sorrows as well as your pleasures they will I trust soften the one and heighten the other feeling

    Adieu

Be resolute for Desse [Attorney to John Westbrook, Harriet Shelley's father] plainly wishes to procrastinate and make out a bill for his worthy (children) patron – How it would please me if old Westbrook were to repent in his last moments and leave all his fortune away from that miserable and odious Eliza [Eliza Westbrook, Harriet Shelley's older sister]

ADDRESS: Percy Bysshe Shelley Esq / Messrs Longdill & Butterfield / 5 Gray's Inn Square / London. POSTMARKS: (1) BATH/17 DE 17 / [1816]: (2) E/ 18 DE 18/ 1816.

Background Notes

A week before this letter was written, on 10 December, the body of Percy Shelley's wife, Harriet Westbrook Shelley, was found in the Serpentine, Hyde Park, in an apparent suicide. By 15 December, a letter from Thomas Hookham, J., had informed Shelley of her death, and he travelled to London to secure custody of his two children from this marriage, Ianthe and Charles (b. 23 June 1813 and 30 November 1814 respectively). However, the Westbrook family refused to give the children to him and took the matter to the Court of Chancery to stop Shelley from ever gaining future custody. This letter of Mary's was written in response to one from Shelley on 16 December, in which he describes the anguish he experienced as a result of these events.

[1] Fanny Imlay committed suicide on 9 October 1816 by taking an overdose of laudanum. Her body was found at the Mackworth Arms Inn, Swansea, Wales.

[2] Marianne Kent Hunt (1788-1857) married Leigh Hunt in 1809. She created profile silhouettes cut out of paper as a hobby.

[3] Here Mary is referring to her forthcoming marriage to Percy, which took place on 30 December Mary at St Mildred's Church in London (with the Godwins as witnesses).

[4] Thomas Jefferson Hogg (1792-1862) and Percy Shelley became friends at Oxford University from which both were expelled in 1811. Hogg was a close friend of Percy and Mary all their lives.

TO LORD BYRON

Bath

January 13th 1817

Dear Lord Byron

Shelley being in London upon business I take upon myself the task & pleasure of informing you that Clare was safely delivered of a little girl yesterday morning (Sunday January 12) at four. She sends her affectionate love to you and begs me to say that she is in excellent [health *crossed out*] spirits and as good health as can be expected. That is to say that she has had a very favourable time and has now no other illness than the weakness incidental to her case.

A letter ought not to be sent so far without a little more news. The people at present are very quiet waiting anxiously for the meeting of parliament – when in the month of March, as Cobbett boldly prophesies a reform will certainly take place [William Cobbett (1763-1835); a radical journalist and politician].

For private news if you feel interest in it, Shelley has become intimate with Leigh Hunt and his family. I have seen them & like Hunt extremely. We have also taken a house in Marlow to which we intend to remove in about two months – And where we dare hope to have the pleasure of your society on your return to England. The town of Marlow is about thirty miles from London.

My little boy is very well and is a very lively child.

It is a long time since Shelley has heard from you and I am sure nothing would give him greater pleasure than to receive news of your motions & enjoyments.

Another incident has also occurred which will surprise you, perhaps. It is a little piece of egotism in me to mention it – but it allows me to sign myself – in assuring you of my esteem & sincere friendship

Mary W. Shelley

ADDRESS: To the Right Honourable / Lord Byron / M. Heutsch-Banquier / Genêve/ Switzerland. POSTMARKS: (1) E/ PAID/ 18 JA I8/ 1817; (2) F 191 [sideways] 17.

TO MARIANNE HUNT

Bath
January 13th 1817

My dear Mrs Hunt

I am going to trouble you with a very impertinent commission – but Mr Shelley's thoughtlessness must be my excuse. Will you be so very kind as to ask him for his dirty linen and send it to the wash for him

If you trouble yourself to answer t[his] impertinent billet will you let me know how your health is and if you take the exercise that you ought. How is Mr Hunt & the dear little children? In a month or six weeks I hope to see you and soon after to be favoured with your promised visit.

Will you also tell me how Mr Shelley continues under the vexation of this hateful business [the Chancery suit for custody of Shelley's children].

Kiss the children for me. & every kind remembrance to Mr H.

Yours very sincerely
Mary W. Shelley

ADDRESS: Mrs. Hunt.

TO PERCY SHELLEY

Bath
Jan 17th 1817

My sweet Love

You were born to be a don Quixote and if that celebrated personage had ever existed except in the brain of Cervantes I should certainly form a theory of transmigration to prove that you lived in Spain some hundred years before & fought with Windmills. You were very good in this except in one thing – which was sitting up all night – which indeed you ought not to do especially when you are so fagged all day.

I wait for the Chancellor's decision with anxiety and yet with great hope – Take care of your own health, sweet, love & all will go well – You wish to be accurate and to give me the very words of Basil M.[1] but unfortunately that was the only part of your letter of which I did not understand a single word – part of it was covered with the seal & the rest nearly illegible

If you have not sent the nipple shield for Clare pray send it without fail by to nights mail as she is in great want of it – send also a pretty book for me. Hunt has some old romances – of King Arthur & the Seven Champions I would take great care of them if he would lend them to me & pray ask Papa for a nice history that I can get here for I am in sad want of books to read in the sick chamber – But pray send the thing for Clare if you have not sent it already which I trust you have. The baby is well.

Blue eyes – gets dearer and sweeter every day – he jumps about like a little squirrel – and stares at the baby with his great eyes –[2]

We have bad weather – & I am when I think at all – in wretched spirits come back with good news my best absent love & we shall be happy – Never before have you been so long away –it is very melancholy. Is Saturday the day certainly – oh that it were past and it were post time Sunday – But I am afraid you will not have time to write much that day – if so pray send a parcel by the mail sunday Enclosing news – & a lb of Green & 2 lb of black tea – for if I have to wait untill teusday I shall be quite sick with expectation

adieu best & dearest – Clare writes to day & directs to Longdills – Have you sent Mrs Hoopers money pray send me word – and if you have not pray do or we shall have another very dangerous visit from Mary H.[3]

send me news of your protegèe [perhaps a reference to Thornton Leigh Hunt (1810–73), the Hunt's precocious eldest child, who spent much time in the poet's company during this period]. Clare writes I entreat you most earnestly & anxiously to take care how you answer it – Be kind but make no promises & above all do not say a word that may imply any responsibility on your part for her future actions – I shall most likely not see your letter but I shall be very anxious for its [ ] contents for you are warmhearted [ ] & indeed sweetest very indiscreet – [ ] pardon this but pray attend to it – Have you given Mrs G. [Godwin] money for your night shirt do not love [lose?] any clothes – dearest adieu be well & happy but remember a white mouses advise–

> Yours tenderly
> M.W.S.

ADDRESS: P. B. Shelley Esq. / Leigh Hunt Esq. / Vale of Health Hampstead / Near London. POSTMARKS: (1) F./ JA 17/ 1817; (2) 10 oClock/ JA. 17/1817 F. Nn.

Background Notes
From 7 October to 7 November 1816, Shelley read *Don Quixote* aloud to Mary Godwin and Claire Clairmont (see Journal Entries and Mary Shelley's Reading List in Bath, p.166)

[1] Basil Montagu (1770–1851), was a prominent attorney and an old friend of Godwin's, and one of Shelley's representatives in the pending Chancery suit.

[2] Blue eyes refers to Mary and Percy's eleven-month-old son, William. The baby he stares at is Claire's newborn daughter, Alba.

[3] Shelley owed £30 to Mrs Hooper, his landlady at Lynmout in 1812.

CHAPTER THREE

Frankenstein Chapter 4 (1818 Edition)

It was on a dreary night of November that I beheld the accomplishment of my toils. With an anxiety that almost amounted to agony, I collected the instruments of life around me, that I might infuse a spark of being into the lifeless thing that lay at my feet. It was already one in the morning; the rain pattered dismally against the panes, and my candle was nearly burnt out, when, by the glimmer of the half-extinguished light, I saw the dull yellow eye of the creature open; it breathed hard, and a convulsive motion agitated its limbs.

How can I describe my emotions at this catastrophe, or how delineate the wretch whom with such infinite pains and care I had endeavoured to form? His limbs were in proportion, and I had selected his features as beautiful. Beautiful! Great God! His yellow skin scarcely covered the work of muscles and arteries beneath; his hair was of a lustrous black, and flowing; his teeth of a pearly whiteness; but these luxuriances only formed a more horrid contrast with his watery eyes, that seemed almost of the same colour as the dun-white sockets in which they were set, his shrivelled complexion and straight black lips.

The different accidents of life are not so changeable as the feelings of human nature. I had worked hard for nearly two years, for the sole purpose of infusing life into an inanimate body. For this I had deprived myself of rest and health. I had desired it with an ardour that far exceeded moderation; but now that I had finished, the beauty of the dream vanished, and breathless horror and disgust filled my heart. Unable to endure the aspect of the being I had created, I rushed out of the room and continued a long time traversing my bed-chamber, unable to compose my mind to sleep. At length lassitude succeeded to the tumult I had before endured, and I threw myself on the bed in my clothes, endeavouring to seek a few moments of forgetfulness. But it was in vain; I slept, indeed, but I was disturbed by the wildest dreams. I thought I saw Elizabeth, in the bloom of health, walking in the streets of Ingolstadt. Delighted and surprised, I embraced her, but as I imprinted the first kiss on her lips, they became livid with the hue of death; her features appeared to change, and I thought that I held the corpse of my dead mother in my arms; a shroud enveloped her form, and I saw the grave-worms crawling in the folds of the flannel. I started from my sleep with horror; a cold dew covered my forehead, my teeth chattered, and every limb became convulsed; when, by the dim and yellow light of the moon, as it forced its way through the window shutters, I beheld the wretch—the miserable monster whom I had created. He held up the curtain of the bed; and his eyes, if eyes they may be called, were fixed on me. His jaws opened, and he muttered some inarticulate sounds, while a grin wrinkled his cheeks. He might have spoken, but I did not hear; one hand was stretched out, seemingly to detain me, but I escaped and rushed downstairs. I took refuge in the courtyard belonging to the house which I inhabited, where I remained during the rest of the night, walking up and down in the greatest agitation, listening attentively, catching and fearing each sound as if it were to announce the approach of the demoniacal corpse to which I had so miserably given life.

Oh! No mortal could support the horror of that countenance. A mummy again endued with animation could not be so hideous as that wretch. I had gazed on him while unfinished; he was ugly then, but when those muscles and joints were rendered capable of motion, it became a thing such as even Dante could not have conceived.

I passed the night wretchedly. Sometimes my pulse beat so quickly and hardly that I felt the palpitation of every artery; at others, I nearly sank to the ground through languor and extreme weakness. Mingled with this horror, I felt the bitterness of disappointment; dreams that had been my food and pleasant rest for so long a space were now become a hell to me; and the change was so rapid, the overthrow so complete!

Morning, dismal and wet, at length dawned and discovered to my sleepless and aching eyes the church of Ingolstadt, its white steeple and clock, which indicated the sixth hour. The porter opened the gates of the court, which had that night been my asylum, and I issued into the streets, pacing them with quick steps, as if I sought to avoid the wretch whom I feared every turning of the street would present to my view. I did not dare return to the apartment which I inhabited, but felt impelled to hurry on, although drenched by the rain which poured from a black and comfortless sky.

I continued walking in this manner for some time, endeavouring by bodily exercise to ease the load that weighed upon my mind. I traversed the streets without any clear conception of where I was or what I was doing. My heart palpitated in the sickness of fear, and I hurried on with irregular steps, not daring to look about me:

> Like one who, on a lonely road,
>   Doth walk in fear and dread,
> And, having once turned round, walks on,
>   And turns no more his head;
> Because he knows a frightful fiend
>   Doth close behind him tread.

[Coleridge's *Ancient Mariner*]

Continuing thus, I came at length opposite to the inn at which the various diligences and carriages usually stopped. Here I paused, I knew not why; but I remained some minutes with my eyes fixed on a coach that was coming towards me from the other end of the street. As it drew nearer I observed that it was the Swiss diligence; it stopped just where I was standing, and on the door being opened, I perceived Henry Clerval, who, on seeing me, instantly sprung out. 'My dear Frankenstein,' exclaimed he, 'how glad I am to see you! How fortunate that you should be here at the very moment of my alighting!'

Nothing could equal my delight on seeing Clerval; his presence brought back to my thoughts my father, Elizabeth, and all those scenes of home so dear to my recollection. I grasped his hand, and in a moment forgot my horror and misfortune; I felt suddenly, and for the first time during many months, calm and serene joy. I welcomed my friend, therefore, in the most cordial manner, and we walked towards my college. Clerval continued talking for some time about our mutual friends and his own good fortune in being permitted to come to Ingolstadt. 'You may easily believe,' said he, 'how great was the difficulty to persuade my father that all necessary knowledge was not comprised in the noble art of book-keeping; and, indeed, I believe I left him incredulous to the last, for his constant answer to my unwearied entreaties was the same as that of the Dutch schoolmaster in *The Vicar of Wakefield*: "I have ten thousand florins a year without Greek, I eat heartily without Greek." But his affection for me at length overcame his dislike of learning, and he has permitted me to undertake a voyage of discovery to the land of knowledge.'

'It gives me the greatest delight to see you; but tell me how you left my father, brothers, and Elizabeth.'

'Very well, and very happy, only a little uneasy that they hear from you so seldom. By the by, I mean to lecture you a little upon their account myself. But, my dear Frankenstein,' continued he, stopping short and gazing full in my face, 'I did not before remark how very ill you appear; so thin and pale; you look as if you had been watching for several nights.'

'You have guessed right; I have lately been so deeply engaged in one occupation that I have not allowed myself sufficient rest, as you see; but I hope, I sincerely hope, that all these employments are now at an end and that I am at length free.'

I trembled excessively; I could not endure to think of, and far less to allude to, the occurrences of the preceding night. I walked with a quick pace, and we soon arrived at my college. I then reflected, and the thought made me shiver, that the creature whom I had left in my apartment might still be there, alive and walking about. I dreaded to behold this monster, but I feared still more that Henry should see him. Entreating him, therefore, to remain a few minutes at the bottom of the stairs, I darted up towards my own room.

My hand was already on the lock of the door before I recollected myself. I then paused, and a cold shivering came over me. I threw the door forcibly open, as children are accustomed to do when they expect a spectre to stand in waiting for them on the other side; but nothing appeared. I stepped fearfully in: the apartment was empty, and my bedroom was also freed from its hideous guest. I could hardly believe that so great a good fortune could have befallen me, but when I became assured that my enemy had indeed fled, I clapped my hands for joy and ran down to Clerval.

We ascended into my room, and the servant presently brought breakfast; but I was unable to contain myself. It was not joy only that possessed me; I felt my flesh tingle with excess of sensitiveness, and my pulse beat rapidly. I was unable to remain for a single instant in the same place; I jumped over the chairs, clapped my hands, and laughed aloud. Clerval at first attributed my unusual spirits to joy on his arrival, but when he observed me more attentively, he saw a wildness in my eyes for which he could not account, and my loud, unrestrained, heartless laughter frightened and astonished him.

'My dear Victor,' cried he, 'what, for God's sake, is the matter? Do not laugh in that manner. How ill you are! What is the cause of all this?'

'Do not ask me,' cried I, putting my hands before my eyes, for I thought I saw the dreaded spectre glide into the room; 'he can tell. Oh, save me! Save me!' I imagined that the monster seized me; I struggled furiously and fell down in a fit.

Poor Clerval! What must have been his feelings? A meeting, which he anticipated with such joy, so strangely turned to bitterness. But I was not the witness of his grief, for I was lifeless and did not recover my senses for a long, long time.

This was the commencement of a nervous fever which confined me for several months. During all that time Henry was my only nurse. I afterwards learned that, knowing my father's advanced age and unfitness for so long a journey, and how wretched my sickness would make Elizabeth, he spared them this grief by concealing the extent of my disorder. He knew that I could not have a more kind and attentive nurse than himself; and, firm in the hope he felt of my recovery, he did not doubt that, instead of doing harm, he performed the kindest action that he could towards them.

But I was in reality very ill, and surely nothing but the unbounded and unremitting attentions of my friend could have restored me to life. The form of the monster on whom I had bestowed existence was for ever before my eyes, and I raved incessantly concerning him. Doubtless my words surprised Henry; he at first believed them to be the wanderings of my disturbed imagination, but the pertinacity with which I continually recurred to the same subject persuaded him that my disorder indeed owed its origin to some uncommon and terrible event.

By very slow degrees, and with frequent relapses that alarmed and grieved my friend, I recovered. I remember the first time I became capable of observing outward objects with any kind of pleasure, I perceived that the fallen leaves had disappeared and that the young buds were shooting forth from the trees that shaded my window. It was a divine spring, and the season contributed greatly to my convalescence. I felt also sentiments of joy and affection revive in my bosom; my gloom disappeared, and in a short time I became as cheerful as before I was attacked by the fatal passion.

'Dearest Clerval,' exclaimed I, 'how kind, how very good you are to me. This whole winter, instead of being spent in study, as you promised yourself, has been consumed in my sick room. How shall I ever repay you? I feel the greatest remorse for the disappointment of which I have been the occasion, but you will forgive me.'

'You will repay me entirely if you do not discompose yourself, but get well as fast as you can; and since you appear in such good spirits, I may speak to you on one subject, may I not?'

I trembled. One subject! What could it be? Could he allude to an object on whom I dared not even think?

'Compose yourself,' said Clerval, who observed my change of colour, 'I will not mention it if it agitates you; but your father and cousin would be very happy if they received a letter from you in your own handwriting. They hardly know how ill you have been and are uneasy at your long silence.'

'Is that all, my dear Henry? How could you suppose that my first thought would not fly towards those dear, dear friends whom I love and who are so deserving of my love?'

'If this is your present temper, my friend, you will perhaps be glad to see a letter that has been lying here some days for you; it is from your cousin, I believe.'

Written in Mary Shelley's lodgings in 5 Abbey Churchyard, Bath.

CHAPTER FOUR

Short Stories
The Mourner

'One fatal remembrance, one sorrow that throws
Its bleak shade alike o'er our joys and our woes,
To which life nothing darker or brighter can bring,
For which joy has no balm, and affliction no sting!'
– MOORE

A gorgeous scene of kingly pride is the prospect now before us! – the offspring of art, the nursling of nature – where can the eye rest on a landscape more deliciously lovely than the fair expanse of Virginia Water, now an open mirror to the sky, now shaded by umbrageous banks, which wind into dark recesses, or are rounded into soft promontories? Looking down on it, now that the sun is low in the west, the eye is dazzled, the soul oppressed, by excess of beauty. Earth, water, air drink to overflowing the radiance that streams from yonder well of light; the foliage of the trees seems dripping with the golden flood; while the lake, filled with no earthly dew, appears but an imbasining of the sun-tinctured atmosphere; and trees and gay pavilion float in its depth, more dear, more distinct than their twins in the upper air. Nor is the scene silent: strains more sweet than those that lull Venus to her balmy rest, more inspiring than the song of Tiresias which awoke Alexander to the deed of ruin, more solemn than the chantings of St. Cecilia, float along the waves and mingle with the lagging breeze, which ruffles not the lake. Strange, that a few dark scores should be the key to this fountain of sound; the unconscious link between unregarded noise and harmonies which unclose paradise to our entranced senses!

The sun touches the extreme boundary, and a softer, milder light mingles a roseate tinge with the fiery glow. Our boat has floated long on the broad expanse; now let it approach the umbrageous bank. The green tresses of the graceful willow dip into the waters, which are checked by them into a ripple. The startled teal dart from their recess, skimming the waves with splashing wing. The stately swans float onward; while innumerable waterfowl cluster together out of the way of the oars. The twilight is blotted by no dark shades; it is one subdued, equal receding of the great tide of day. We may disembark, and wander yet amid the glades, long before the thickening shadows speak of night. The plantations are formed of every English tree, with an old oak or two standing out in the walks. There the glancing foliage obscures heaven, as the silken texture of a veil a woman's lovely features. Beneath such fretwork we may indulge in light-hearted thoughts; or, if sadder meditations lead us to seek darker shades, we may pass the cascade towards the large groves of pine, with their vast undergrowth of laurel, reaching up to the Belvidere; or, on the opposite side of the water, sit under the shadow of the silver-stemmed birch, or beneath the leafy pavilions of those fine old beeches, whose high fantastic roots seem formed in nature's sport; and the near jungle of sweet-smelling myrica leaves no sense unvisited by pleasant ministration.

Now this splendid scene is reserved for the royal possessor; but in past years; while the lodge was called the Regent's Cottage, or before, when the under-ranger inhabited it, the mazy paths of Chapel Wood were open, and the iron gates enclosing the plantations and Virginia Water were guarded by no Cerebus untamable by sops. It was here, on a summer's evening, that Horace Neville and his two fair cousins floated idly on the placid lake, 'In that sweet mood when pleasant thoughts Bring sad thoughts to the mind.'

Neville had been eloquent in praise of English scenery. 'In distant climes,' he said, 'we may find landscapes grand in barbaric wildness, or rich in the luxuriant vegetation of the south, or sublime in Alpine magnificence. We may lament, though it is ungrateful to say so on such a night as this, the want of a more genial sky; but where find scenery to be compared to the verdant, well-wooded, well-watered groves of our native land; the clustering cottages, shadowed by fine old elms; each garden blooming with early flowers, each lattice gay with geraniums and roses; the blue-eyed child devouring his white bread, while he drives a cow to graze; the hedge redolent with summer blooms; the enclosed cornfields, seas of golden grain, weltering in the breeze; the stile, the track across the meadow, leading through the copse, under which the path winds, and the meeting branches overhead, which give, by their dimming tracery, a cathedral-like solemnity to the scene; the river, winding "with sweet inland murmur;" and, as additional graces, spots like these – oases of taste – gardens of Eden – the works of wealth, which evince at once the greatest power and the greatest will to create beauty?'

'And yet,' continued Neville, 'it was with difficulty that I persuaded myself to reap the best fruits of my uncle's will, and to inhabit this spot, familiar to my boyhood, associated with unavailing regrets and recollected pain.'

Horace Neville was a man of birth – of wealth; but he could hardly be termed a man of the world. There was in his nature a gentleness, a sweetness, a winning sensibility, allied to talent and personal distinction, that gave weight to his simplest expressions, and excited sympathy for all his emotions. His younger cousin, his junior by several years, was attached to him by the tenderest sentiments – secret long – but they were now betrothed to each other – a lovely, happy pair. She looked inquiringly, but he turned away. 'No more of this,' he said, and, giving a swifter impulse to their boat, they speedily reached the shore, landed, and walked through the long extent of Chapel Wood. It was dark night before they met their carriage at Bishopsgate.

A week or two after, Horace received letters to call him to a distant part of the country. A few days before his departure, he requested his cousin to walk with him. They bent their steps across several meadows to Old Windsor Churchyard. At first he did not deviate from the usual path; and as they went they talked cheerfully – gaily. The beauteous sunny day might well exhilarate them; the dancing waves sped onwards at their feet; the country church lifted its rustic spire into the bright pure sky. There was nothing in their conversation that could induce his cousin to think that Neville had led her hither for any saddening purpose; but when they were about to quit the churchyard, Horace, as if he had suddenly recollected himself, turned from the path, crossed the greensward, and paused beside a grave near the river. No stone was there to commemorate the being who reposed beneath – it was thickly grown with grass, starred by a luxuriant growth of humble daisies: a few dead leaves, a broken bramble twig, defaced its neatness. Neville removed these, and then said, 'Juliet, I commit this sacred spot to your keeping while I am away.'

'There is no monument,' he continued: 'for her commands were implicitly obeyed by the two beings to whom she addressed them. One day another may lie near, and his name will be her epitaph. I do not mean myself,' he said, half-smiling at the terror his cousin's countenance expressed; 'but promise me, Juliet, to preserve this grave from every violation. I do not wish to sadden you by the story; yet, if I have excited your interest, I will satisfy it; but not now – not here.'

It was not till the following day, when, in company with her sister, they again visited Virginia Water. Seated under the shadow of its pines, whose melodious swinging in the wind breathed unearthly harmony, Neville, unasked, commenced his story.

'I was sent to Eton at eleven years of age. I will not dwell upon my sufferings there; I would hardly refer to them, did they not make a part of my present narration. I was a fag to a hard taskmaster; every labour he could invent – and the youthful tyrant was ingenious – he devised for my annoyance; early and late, I was forced to be in attendance, to the neglect of my school duties, so incurring punishment. There were worse things to bear than these: it was his delight to put me to shame, and, finding that I had too much of my mother in my blood – to endeavour to compel me to acts of cruelty from which my nature revolted – I refused to obey. Speak of West Indian slavery! I hope things may be better now; in my days, the tender years of aristocratic childhood were yielded up to a capricious, unrelenting, cruel bondage, far beyond the measured despotism of Jamaica.

'One day – I had been two years at school, and was nearly thirteen – my tyrant, I will give him no other name, issued a command, in the wantonness of power, for me to destroy a poor little bullfinch I had tamed and caged. In a hapless hour he found it in my room, and was indignant that I should dare to appropriate a single pleasure. I refused, stubbornly, dauntlessly, though the consequence of my disobedience was immediate and terrible. At this moment a message came from my tormentor's tutor – his father had arrived. "Well, old lad," he cried, "I shall pay you off some day!" Seizing my pet at the same time, he wrung its neck, threw it at my feet, and, with a laugh of derision, quitted the room.

'Never before – never may I again feel the same swelling, boiling fury in my bursting heart; – the sight of my nursling expiring at my feet – my desire of vengeance – my impotence, created a Vesuvius within me, that no tears flowed to quench. Could I have uttered – acted – my passion, it would have been less torturous: it was so when I burst into a torrent of abuse and imprecation. My vocabulary – it must have been a choice collection – was supplied by him against whom it was levelled. But words were air. I desired to give more substantial proof of my resentment – I destroyed everything in the room belonging to him; I tore them to pieces, I stamped on them, crushed them with more than childish strength. My last act was to seize a timepiece, on which my tyrant infinitely prided himself, and to dash it to the ground. The sight of this, as it lay shattered at my feet, recalled me to my senses, and something like an emotion of fear allayed the tumult in my heart. I began to meditate an escape: I got out of the house, ran down a lane, and across some meadows, far out of bounds, above Eton. I was seen by an elder boy, a friend of my tormentor. He called to me, thinking at first that I was performing some errand for him; but seeing that I "shirked", he repeated his "Come up!" in an authoritative voice. It put wings to my heels; he did not deem it necessary to pursue. But I grow tedious, my dear Juliet; enough that fears the most intense, of punishment both from my masters and the upper boys, made me resolve to run away. I reached the banks of the Thames, tied my clothes over my head, swam across, and, traversing several fields, entered Windsor Forest, with a vague childish feeling of being able to hide myself for ever in the unexplored obscurity of its immeasurable wilds. It was early autumn; the weather was mild, even warm; the forest oaks yet showed no sign of winter change, though the fern beneath wore a yellowy tinge. I got within Chapel Wood; I fed upon chestnuts and beechnuts; I continued to hide myself from the gamekeepers and woodmen. I lived thus two days.

'But chestnuts and beechnuts were sorry fare to a growing lad of thirteen years old. A day's rain occurred, and I began to think myself the most unfortunate boy on record. I had a distant, obscure idea of starvation: I thought of the Children in the Wood, of their leafy shroud, gift of the pious robin; this brought my poor bullfinch to my mind, and tears streamed in torrents down my cheeks. I thought of my father and mother; of you, then my little baby cousin and playmate; and I cried with renewed fervour, till, quite exhausted, I curled myself up under a huge oak among some dry leaves, the relics of a hundred summers, and fell asleep.

'I ramble on in my narration as if I had a story to tell; yet I have little except a portrait – a sketch – to present, for your amusement or interest. When I awoke, the first object that met my opening eyes was a little foot, delicately clad in silk and soft kid. I looked up in dismay, expecting to behold some gaily dressed appendage to this indication of high-bred elegance; but I saw a girl, perhaps seventeen, simply clad in a dark cotton dress, her face shaded by a large, very coarse straw hat; she was pale even to marmoreal whiteness; her chestnut-coloured hair was parted in plain tresses across a brow which wore traces of extreme suffering; her eyes were blue, full, large, melancholy, often even suffused with tears; but her mouth had an infantine sweetness and innocence in its expression, that softened the otherwise sad expression of her countenance.

'She spoke to me. I was too hungry, too exhausted, too unhappy, to resist her kindness, and gladly permitted her to lead me to her home. We passed out of the wood by some broken palings on to Bishopsgate Heath, and after no long walk arrived at her habitation. It was a solitary, dreary-looking cottage; the palings were in disrepair, the garden waste, the lattices unadorned by flowers or creepers; within, all was neat, but sombre, and even mean. The diminutiveness of a cottage requires an appearance of cheerfulness and elegance to make it pleasing; the bare floor, – clean, it is true, – the rush chairs, deal table, checked curtains of this cot, were beneath even a peasant's rusticity; yet it was the dwelling of my lovely guide, whose little white hand, delicately gloved, contrasted with her unadorned attire, as did her gentle self with the clumsy appurtenances of her too humble dwelling.

'Poor child! she had meant entirely to hide her origin, to degrade herself to a peasant's state, and little thought that she for ever betrayed herself by the strangest incongruities. Thus, the arrangements of her table were mean, her fare meagre for a hermit; but the linen was matchlessly fine, and wax lights stood in candlesticks which a beggar would almost have disdained to own. But I talk of circumstances I observed afterwards; then

I was chiefly aware of the plentiful breakfast she caused her single attendant, a young girl, to place before me, and of the sweet soothing voice of my hostess, which spoke a kindness with which lately I had been little conversant. When my hunger was appeased, she drew my story from me, encouraged me to write to my father, and kept me at her abode till, after a few days, I returned to school pardoned. No long time elapsed before I got into the upper forms, and my woful slavery ended.

'Whenever I was able, I visited my disguised nymph. I no longer associated with my schoolfellows; their diversions, their pursuits appeared vulgar and stupid to me; I had but one object in view – to accomplish my lessons, and to steal to the cottage of Ellen Burnet.

'Do not look grave, love! true, others as young as I then was have loved, and I might also; but not Ellen. Her profound, her intense melancholy, sister to despair – her serious, sad discourse – her mind, estranged from all worldly concerns, forbade that; but there was an enchantment in her sorrow, a fascination in her converse, that lifted me above commonplace existence; she created a magic circle, which I entered as holy ground: it was not akin to heaven, for grief was the presiding spirit; but there was an exaltation of sentiment, an enthusiasm, a view beyond the grave, which made it unearthly, singular, wild, enthralling. You have often observed that I strangely differ from all other men; I mingle with them, make one in their occupations and diversions, but I have a portion of my being sacred from them: – a living well, sealed up from their contamination, lies deep in my heart – it is of little use, but there it is; Ellen opened the spring, and it has flowed ever since.

'Of what did she talk? She recited no past adventures, alluded to no past intercourse with friend or relative; she spoke of the various woes that wait on humanity, on the intricate mazes of life, on the miseries of passion, of love, remorse, and death, and that which we may hope or fear beyond the tomb; she spoke of the sensation of wretchedness alive in her own broken heart, and then she grew fearfully eloquent, till, suddenly pausing, she reproached herself for making me familiar with such wordless misery. "I do you harm," she often said; "I unfit you for society; I have tried, seeing you thrown upon yonder distorted miniature of a bad world, to estrange you from its evil contagion; I fear that I shall be the cause of greater harm to you than could spring from association with your fellow-creatures in the ordinary course of things. This is not well – avoid the stricken deer."

'There were darker shades in the picture than those which I have already developed. Ellen was more miserable than the imagination of one like you, dear girl, unacquainted with woe, can portray. Sometimes she gave words to her despair – it was so great as to confuse the boundary between physical and mental sensation – and every pulsation of her heart was a throb of pain. She has suddenly broken off in talking of her sorrows, with a cry of agony – bidding me leave her – hiding her face on her arms, shivering with the anguish some thought awoke. The idea that chiefly haunted her, though she earnestly endeavoured to put it aside, was self-destruction – to snap the silver cord that bound together so much grace, wisdom, and sweetness – to rob the world of a creation made to be its ornament. Sometimes her piety checked her; oftener a sense of unendurable suffering made her brood with pleasure over the dread resolve. She spoke of it to me as being wicked; yet I often fancied this was done rather to prevent her example from being of ill effect to me, than from any conviction that the Father of all would regard angrily the last act of His miserable child. Once she had prepared the mortal beverage; it was on the table before her when I entered; she did not deny its nature, she did not attempt to justify herself; she only besought me not to hate her, and to soothe by my kindness her last moments. – "I cannot live!" was all her explanation, all her excuse; and it was spoken with such fervent wretchedness that it seemed wrong to attempt to persuade her to prolong the sense of pain. I did not act like a boy; I wonder I did not; I made one simple request, to which she instantly acceded, that she should walk with me to this Belvidere. It was a glorious sunset; beauty and the spirit of love breathed in the wind, and hovered over the softened hues of the landscape. "Look, Ellen," I cried, "if only such loveliness of nature existed, it were worth living for!"

"'True, if a latent feeling did not blot this glorious scene with murky shadows. Beauty is as we see it – my eyes view all things deformed and evil." She closed them as she said this; but, young and sensitive, the visitings of the soft breeze already began to minister consolation. "Dearest Ellen," I continued, "what do I not owe to you? I am your boy, your pupil; I might have gone on blindly as others do, but you opened my eyes; you have given me a sense of the just, the good, the beautiful – and have you done this merely for my misfortune? If you leave me, what can become of me?" The last words came from my heart, and tears gushed from my eyes. "Do not leave me, Ellen," I said; "I cannot live without you – and I cannot die, for I have a mother – a father." She turned quickly round, saying, "You are blessed sufficiently." Her voice struck me as unnatural; she grew deadly pale as she spoke, and was obliged to sit down. Still I clung to her, prayed, cried; till she – I had never seen her shed a tear before – burst into passionate weeping. After this she seemed to forget her resolve. We returned by moonlight, and our talk was even more calm and cheerful than usual. When in her cottage, I poured away the fatal draught. Her "good-night" bore with it no traces of her late agitation; and the next day she said, "I have thoughtlessly, even wickedly, created a new duty to myself, even at a time when I had forsworn all; but I will be true to it. Pardon me for making you familiar with emotions and scenes so dire; I will behave better – I will preserve myself if I can, till the link between us is loosened, or broken, and I am free again."

'One little incident alone occurred during our intercourse that appeared at all to connect her with the world. Sometimes I brought her a newspaper, for those were stirring times; and though, before I knew her, she had forgotten all except the world her own heart enclosed, yet, to please me, she would talk of Napoleon – Russia, from whence the emperor now returned overthrown – and the prospect of his final defeat. The paper lay one day on her table; some words caught her eye; she bent eagerly down to read them, and her bosom heaved with violent palpitation; but she subdued herself, and after a few moments told me to take the paper away. Then, indeed, I did feel an emotion of even impertinent inquisitiveness; I found nothing to satisfy it – though afterwards I became aware that it contained a singular advertisement, saying, "If these lines meet the eye of any one of the passengers who were on board the St. Mary, bound for Liverpool from Barbadoes, which sailed on the third of May last, and was destroyed by fire in the high seas, a part of the crew only having been saved by his Majesty's frigate the Bellerophon, they are entreated to communicate with the advertiser; and if any one be acquainted with the particulars of the Hon. Miss Eversham's fate and present abode, they are earnestly requested to disclose them, directing to L. E., Stratton Street, Park Lane."

'It was after this event, as winter came on, that symptoms of decided ill-health declared themselves in the delicate frame of my poor Ellen. I have often suspected that, without positively attempting her life, she did many things that tended to abridge it and to produce mortal disease. Now, when really ill, she refused all medical attendance; but she got better again, and I thought her nearly well when I saw her for the last time, before going home for the Christmas holidays. Her manner was full of affection: she relied, she said, on the continuation of my friendship; she made me promise never to forget her, though she refused to write to me, and forbade any letters from me.

'Even now I see her standing at her humble doorway. If an appearance of illness and suffering can ever he termed lovely, it was in her. Still she was to be viewed as the wreck of beauty. What must she not have been in happier days, with her angel expression of face, her nymph-like figure, her voice, whose tones were music? "So young – so lost!" was the sentiment that burst even from me, a young lad, as I waved my hand to her as a last adieu. She hardly looked more than fifteen, but none could doubt that her very soul was impressed by the sad lines of sorrow that rested so unceasingly on her fair brow. Away from her, her figure for ever floated before my eyes; – I put my hands before them, still she was there: my day, my night dreams were filled by my recollections of her.

'During the winter holidays, on a fine soft day, I went out to hunt: you, dear Juliet, will remember the sad catastrophe; I fell and broke my leg. The only person who saw me fall was a young man who rode one of the most beautiful horses I ever saw, and I believe it was by watching him as he took a leap, that I incurred my disaster: he dismounted, and was at my side in a minute. My own animal had fled; he called his; it obeyed his voice; with ease he lifted my light figure on to the saddle, contriving to support my leg, and so conducted me a short distance to a lodge situated in the woody recesses of Elmore Park, the seat of the Earl of D – , whose second son my preserver was. He was my sole nurse for a day or two, and during the whole of my illness passed many hours of each day by my bedside. As I lay gazing on him, while he read to me, or talked, narrating a thousand stranger adventures which had occurred during his service in the Peninsula, I thought – is it for ever to be my fate to fall in with the highly gifted and excessively unhappy?

'The immediate neighbour of Lewis' family was Lord Eversham. He had married in very early youth, and became a widower young. After this misfortune, which passed like a deadly blight over his prospects and possessions, leaving the gay view utterly sterile and bare, he left his surviving infant daughter under the care of Lewis' mother, and travelled for many years in far distant lands. He returned when Clarice was about ten, a lovely sweet child, the pride and delight of all connected with her. Lord Eversham, on his return – he was then hardly more than thirty – devoted himself to her education. They were never separate: he was a good musician, and she became a proficient under his tutoring. They rode – walked – read together. When a father is all that a father may be, the sentiments of filial piety, entire dependence, and perfect confidence being united, the love of a daughter is one of the deepest and strongest, as it is the purest passion of which our natures are capable. Clarice worshipped her parent, who came, during the transition from mere childhood to the period when reflection and observation awaken, to adorn a commonplace existence with all the brilliant adjuncts which enlightened and devoted affection can bestow. He appeared to her like an especial gift of Providence, a guardian angel – but far dearer, as being akin to her own nature. She grew, under his eye, in loveliness and refinement both of intellect and heart.

These feelings were not divided – almost strengthened, by the engagement that had taken place between her and Lewis: – Lewis was destined for the army, and, after a few years' service, they were to be united.

'It is hard, when all is fair and tranquil, when the world, opening before the ardent gaze of youth, looks like a well-kept demesne, unencumbered by let or hindrance for the annoyance of the young traveller, that we should voluntarily stray into desert wilds and tempest-visited districts. Lewis Elmore was ordered to Spain; and, at the same time, Lord Eversham found it necessary to visit some estates he possessed in Barbadoes. He was not sorry to revisit a scene, which had dwelt in his memory as an earthly paradise, nor to show to his daughter a new and strange world, so to form her understanding and enlarge her mind. They were to return in three months, and departed as on a summer tour. Clarice was glad that, while her lover gathered experience and knowledge in a distant land, she should not remain in idleness; she was glad that there would be some diversion for her anxiety during his perilous absence; and in every way she enjoyed the idea of travelling with her beloved father, who would fill every hour, and adorn every new scene, with pleasure and delight. They sailed. Clarice wrote home, with enthusiastic expressions of rapture and delight, from Madeira: – yet, without her father, she said, the fair scene had been blank to her. More than half her letter was filled by the expressions of her gratitude and affection for her adored and revered parent. While he, in his, with fewer words, perhaps, but with no less energy, spoke of his satisfaction in her improvement, his pride in her beauty, and his grateful sense of her love and kindness.

'Such were they, a matchless example of happiness in the dearest connection in life, as resulting from the exercise of their reciprocal duties and affections. A father and daughter; the one all care, gentleness, and sympathy, consecrating his life for her happiness; the other fond, duteous, grateful: – such had they been, – and where were they now, – the noble, kind, respected parent, and the beloved and loving child! They had departed from England as on a pleasure voyage down an inland stream; but the ruthless car of destiny had overtaken them on their unsuspecting way, crushing them under its heavy wheels – scattering love, hope, and joy as the bellowing avalanche overwhelms and grinds to mere spray the streamlet of the valley. They were gone; but whither? Mystery hung over the fate of the most helpless victim; and my friend's anxiety was, to penetrate the clouds that hid poor Clarice from his sight.

'After an absence of a few months, they had written, fixing their departure in the St. Mary, to sail from Barbadoes in a few days. Lewis, at the same time, returned from Spain: he was invalided, in his very first action, by a bad wound in his side. He arrived, and each day expected to hear of the landing of his friends, when that common messenger, the newspaper, brought him tidings to fill him with more than anxiety – with fear and agonising doubt. The St. Mary had caught fire, and had burned in the open sea. A frigate, the Bellerophon, had saved a part of the crew. In spite of illness and a physician's commands, Lewis set out the same day for London to ascertain as speedily as possible the fate of her he loved. There he heard that the frigate was expected in the Downs. Without alighting from his travelling chaise, he posted thither, arriving in a burning fever. He went on board, saw the commander, and spoke with the crew. They could give him few particulars as to whom they had saved; they had touched at Liverpool, and left there most of the persons, including all the passengers rescued from the St. Mary. Physical suffering for awhile disabled Mr. Elmore; he was confined by his wound and consequent fever, and only recovered to give himself up to his exertions to discover the fate of his friends; – they did not appear nor write; and all Lewis' inquiries only tended to confirm his worst fears; yet still he hoped, and still continued indefatigable in his perquisitions. He visited Liverpool and Ireland, whither some of the passengers had gone, and learnt only scattered, incongruous details of the fearful tragedy, that told nothing of Miss Eversham's present abode, though much that confirmed his suspicion that she still lived.

'The fire on board the St. Mary had raged long and fearfully before the Bellerophon hove in sight, and boats came off for the rescue of the crew. The women were to be first embarked; but Clarice clung to her father, and refused to go till he should accompany her. Some fearful presentiment that, if she were saved, he would remain and die, gave such energy to her resolve, that not the entreaties of her father, nor the angry expostulations of the captain, could shake it. Lewis saw this man, after the lapse of two or three months, and he threw most light on the dark scene. He well remembered that, transported with anger by her obstinacy, he had said to her, "You will cause your father's death – and be as much a parricide as if you put poison into his cup; you are not the first girl who has murdered her father in her wilful mood." Still Clarice passionately refused to go – there was no time for long parley – the point was yielded, and she remained pale, but firm, near her parent, whose arm was around her, supporting her during the awful interval. It was no period for regular action and calm order; a tempest was rising, the scorching waves blew this way and that, making a fearful day of the night which veiled all except the burning ship. The boats returned with difficulty, and one only could contrive to approach; it was nearly full; Lord Eversham and his daughter advanced to the deck's edge to get in. "We can only take one of you," vociferated the sailors; "keep back on your life! throw the girl to us – we will come back for you if we can." Lord Eversham cast with a strong arm his daughter, who had now entirely lost her self-possession, into the boat; she was alive again in a minute; she called to her father, held out her arms to him, and would have thrown herself into the sea, but was held back by the sailors. Meanwhile Lord Eversham, feeling that no boat could again approach the lost vessel, contrived to heave a spar overboard, and threw himself into the sea, clinging to it. The boat, tossed by the huge waves, with difficulty made its way to the frigate; and as it rose from the trough of the sea, Clarice saw her father struggling with his fate – battling with the death that at last became the victor; the spar floated by, his arms had fallen from it; were those his pallid features? She neither wept nor fainted, but her limbs grew rigid, her face colourless, and she was lifted as a log on to the deck of the frigate.

'The captain allowed that on her homeward voyage the people had rather a horror of her, as having caused her father's death; her own servants had perished, few people remembered who she was; but they talked together with no careful voices as they passed her, and a hundred times she must have heard herself accused of having destroyed her parent. She spoke to no one, or only in brief reply when addressed; to avoid the rough remonstrances of those around, she appeared at table, ate as well as she could; but there was a settled wretchedness in her face that never changed. When they landed at Liverpool, the captain conducted her to an hotel; he left her, meaning to return, but an opportunity of sailing that night for the Downs occurred, of which he availed himself, without again visiting her. He knew, he said, and truly, that she was in her native country, where she had but to write a letter to gather crowds of friends about her; and where can greater civility be found than at an English hotel, if it is known that you are perfectly able to pay your bill?

'This was all that Mr. Elmore could learn, and it took many months to gather together these few particulars. He went to the hotel at Liverpool. It seemed that as soon as there appeared some hope of rescue from the frigate, Lord Eversham had given his pocket-book to his daughter's care, containing bills on a banking-house at Liverpool to the amount of a few hundred pounds. On the second day after Clarice's arrival there, she had sent for the master of the hotel, and showed him these. He got the cash for her; and the next day she quitted Liverpool in a little coasting vessel. In vain Lewis endeavoured to trace her. Apparently she had crossed to Ireland; but whatever she had done, wherever she had gone, she had taken infinite pains to conceal herself, and all due was speedily lost.

'Lewis had not yet despaired; he was even now perpetually making journeys, sending emissaries, employing every possible means for her discovery. From the moment he told me this story, we talked of nothing else. I became deeply interested, and we ceaselessly discussed the probabilities of the case, and where she might be concealed. That she did not meditate suicide was evident from her having possessed herself of money; yet, unused to the world, young, lovely, and inexperienced, what could be her plan? What might not have been her fate?

'Meanwhile I continued for nearly three months confined by the fracture of my limb; before the lapse of that time, I had begun to crawl about the ground, and now I considered myself as nearly recovered. It had been settled that I should not return to Eton, but be entered at Oxford; and this leap from boyhood to man's estate elated me considerably. Yet still I thought of my poor Ellen, and was angry at her obstinate silence. Once or twice I had, disobeying her command, written to her, mentioning my accident, and the kind attentions of Mr. Elmore. Still she wrote not; and I began to fear that her illness might have had a fatal termination. She had made me vow so solemnly never to mention her name, never to inquire about her during my absence, that, considering obedience the first duty of a young inexperienced boy to one older than himself, I resisted each suggestion of my affection or my fears to transgress her orders.

'And now spring came, with its gift of opening buds, odoriferous flowers, and sunny genial days. I returned home, and found my family on the eve of their departure for London; my long confinement had weakened me; it was deemed inadvisable for me to encounter the bad air and fatigues of the metropolis, and I remained to rusticate. I rode and hunted, and thought of Ellen; missing the excitement of her conversation, and feeling a vacancy in my heart which she had filled. I began to think of riding across the country from Shropshire to Berks for the purpose of seeing her. The whole landscape haunted my imagination – the fields round Eton – the silver Thames – the majestic forest – this lovely scene of Virginia Water – the heath and her desolate cottage – she herself pale, slightly bending from weakness of health, awakening from dark abstraction to bestow on me a kind smile of welcome. It grew into a passionate desire of my heart to behold her, to cheer her as I might by my affectionate attentions, to hear her, and to hang upon her accents of inconsolable despair as if it had been celestial harmony. As I meditated on these things, a voice seemed for ever to repeat, Now go, or it will be too late; while another yet more mournful tone responded, You can never see her more!

'I was occupied by these thoughts, as, on a summer moonlight night, I loitered in the shrubbery, unable to quit a scene of entrancing beauty, when I was startled at hearing myself called by Mr. Elmore. He came on his way to the coast; he had received a letter from Ireland, which made him think that Miss Eversham was residing near Enniscorthy, – a strange place for her to select, but as concealment was evidently her object, not an improbable one. Yet his hopes were not high; on the contrary, he performed this journey more from the resolve to leave nothing undone, than in expectation of a happy result. He asked me if I would accompany him; I was delighted with the offer, and we departed together on the following morning.

'We arrived at Milford Haven, where we were to take our passage. The packet was to sail early in the morning – we walked on the beach, and beguiled the time by talk. I had never mentioned Ellen to Lewis; I felt now strongly inclined to break my vow, and to relate my whole adventure with her; but restrained myself, and we spoke only of the unhappy Clarice – of the despair that must have been hers, of her remorse and unavailing regret.

'We retired to rest; and early in the morning I was called to prepare for going on board. I got ready, and then knocked at Lewis' door; he admitted me, for he was dressed, though a few of his things were still unpacked, and scattered about the room. The morocco case of a miniature was on his table; I took it up. "Did I never show you that?" said Elmore; "poor dear Clarice! she was very happy when that was painted!"

'I opened it; – rich, luxuriant curls clustered on her brow and the snow-white throat; there was a light zephyr appearance in the figure; an expression of unalloyed exuberant happiness in the countenance; but those large dove's eyes, the innocence that dwelt on her mouth, could not be mistaken, and the name of Ellen Burnet burst from my lips.

'There was no doubt: why had I ever doubted? The thing was so plain! Who but the survivor of such a parent, and she the apparent cause of his death, could be so miserable as Ellen? A torrent of explanation followed, and a thousand minute circumstances, forgotten before, now assured us that my sad hermitess was the beloved of Elmore. No more sea voyage – not a second of delay – our chaise, the horses' heads turned to the east, rolled on with lightning rapidity, yet far too slowly to satisfy our impatience. It was not until we arrived at Worcester that the tide of expectation, flowing all one way, ebbed. Suddenly, even while I was telling Elmore some anecdote to prove that, in spite of all, she would be accessible to consolation, I remembered her ill-health and my fears. Lewis saw the change my countenance underwent; for some time I could not command my voice; and when at last I spoke, my gloomy anticipations passed like an electric shock into my friend's soul.

'When we arrived at Oxford we halted for an hour or two, unable to proceed; yet we did not converse on the subject so near our hearts, nor until we arrived in sight of Windsor did a word pass between us; then Elmore said, "To-morrow morning, dear Neville, you shall visit Clarice; we must not be too precipitate."

'The morrow came. I arose with that intolerable weight at my breast, which it is grief's worst heritage to feel. A sunny day it was; yet the atmosphere looked black to me; my heart was dead within me. We sat at the breakfast-table, but neither ate, and after some restless indecision, we left our inn, and (to protract the interval) walked to Bishopsgate. Our conversation belied our feelings: we spoke as if we expected all to be well; we felt that there was no hope. We crossed the heath along the accustomed path. On one side was the luxuriant foliage of the forest, on the other the widespread moor; her cottage was situated at one extremity, and could hardly be distinguished, until we should arrive close to it. When we drew near, Lewis bade me go on alone; he would wait my return. I obeyed, and reluctantly approached the confirmation of my fears. At length it stood before me, the lonely cot and desolate garden; the unfastened wicket swung in the breeze; every shutter was closed.

'To stand motionless and gaze on these symbols of my worst forebodings was all that I could do. My heart seemed to me to call aloud for Ellen, – for such was she to me, – her other name might be a fiction – but silent as her own life-deserted lips were mine. Lewis grew impatient, and advanced. My stay had occasioned a transient ray of hope to enter his mind; it vanished when he saw me and her deserted dwelling. Slowly we turned away, and were directing our steps back again, when my name was called by a child. A little girl came running across some fields towards us, whom at last I recognised as having seen before with Ellen. "Mr. Neville, there is a letter for you!" cried the child. "A letter; where? – who?" "The lady left a letter for you. You must go to Old Windsor, to Mr. Cooke's; he has got it for you."

'She had left a letter: was she then departed on an earthly journey? "I will go for it immediately. Mr. Cooke! Old Windsor!

where shall I find him? who is he?" "Oh, sir, everybody knows him," said the child; "he lives close to the churchyard; he is the sexton. After the burial, Nancy gave him the letter to take care of."

'Had we hoped? had we for a moment indulged the expectation of ever again seeing our miserable friend? Never! O never! Our hearts had told us that the sufferer was at peace – the unhappy orphan with her father in the abode of spirits! Why, then, were we here? Why had a smile dwelt on our lips, now wreathed into the expression of anguish? Our full hearts demanded one consolation – to weep upon her grave; her sole link now with us, her mourners. There at last my boy's grief found vent in tears, in lamentation. You saw the spot; the grassy mound rests lightly on the bosom of fair Clarice, of my own poor Ellen. Stretched upon this, kissing the scarcely springing turf; for many hours no thought visited me but the wretched one, that she had lived, and was lost to me for ever!

'If Lewis had ever doubted the identity of my friend with her he loved, the letter put into our hands undeceived him; the handwriting was Miss Eversham's, it was directed to me, and contained words like these: – "April 11."

"'I have vowed never to mention certain beloved names, never to communicate with beings who cherished me once, to whom my deepest gratitude is due; and, as well as poor bankrupt can, is paid. Perhaps it is a mere prevarication to write to you, dear Horace, concerning them; but Heaven pardon me! my disrobed spirit would not repose, I fear, if I did not thus imperfectly bid them a last farewell.

"'You know him, Neville; and know that he for ever laments her whom he has lost. Describe your poor Ellen to him, and he will speedily see that she died on the waves of the murderous Atlantic. Ellen had nothing in common with her, save love for, and interest in him. Tell him it had been well for him, perhaps, to have united himself to the child of prosperity, the nursling of deep love; but it had been destruction, even could he have meditated such an act, to wed the parrici – .

"'I will not write that word. Sickness and near death have taken the sting from my despair. The agony of woe which you witnessed is melted into tender affliction and pious hope. I am not miserable now. Now! When you read these words, the hand that writes, the eye that sees, will be a little dust, becoming one with the earth around it. You, perhaps he, will visit my quiet retreat, bestow a few tears on my fate, but let them be secret; they may make green my grave, but do not let a misplaced feeling adorn it with any other tribute. It is my last request; let no stone, no name, mark that spot.

"'Farewell, dear Horace! Farewell to one other whom I may not name. May the God to whom I am about to resign my spirit in confidence and hope, bless your earthly career! Blindly, perhaps, you will regret me for your own sakes; but for mine, you will be grateful to the Providence which has snapt the heavy chain binding me to unutterable sorrow, and which permits me from my lowly grass-grown tomb to say to you, I am at peace.

"'ELLEN.'"

The Swiss Peasant

Why is the mind of man so apt to be swayed by contraries? Why does the imagination for ever paint the impossible in glittering tints, and the hearts of wayward mortals cling, with the greatest tenacity, to what, eel-like, is bent on escaping from their grasp? Why – to bring the matter home – is solitude abhorrent to me, now that I enjoy it in perfection? I have apostrophised the coy nymph in ball-rooms, when the bright lamps of heaven were shamed by brighter earth-stars, and lamented her absence at a picnic party, where the nightingale was silenced by the fiddle.

And now, O solitude! I abjure thee, in thy fitting temple – in Switzerland – among cloud-piercing mountains, by the resounding waves of the isle-surrounding lake. I am beside the waters of Uri – where Tell lived – in Brunen, where the Swiss patriots swore to die for freedom. It rains – magic word to destroy the spell to which these words give rise – the clouds envelop the hills – the white mists veil the ravines – there is a roar and a splash in my ears – and now and then the vapours break and scatter themselves, and I see something dark between, which is the hoar side of a dark precipice, but which might as well be the turf stack or old wall that bounded Cumberland's view as he wrote the *Wheel of Fortune*.

The sole book that I possess is the *Prisoner of Chillon*. I have read it through three times within an hour. Its noble author composed it to beguile weary hours like these when he remained rain-bound for three days in a little inn on the shores of the Lake of Geneva; and cannot I, following with unequal steps, so cheat the minutes in this dim spot? I never, by the by, could invent the commonest incident. As a man of honour, of course I never lie; but, as a nursery child and schoolboy, I never did; simply, as I remember, because I never could concoct one; – but a true tale was lately narrated to me by its very heroine, the incidents of which haunt my memory, adorned as they were by her animated looks and soft silvery accent. Let me try to record them, stripped though they must be of their greatest charm.

I was, but a week ago, travelling with my friend Ashburn in a coupée, in the district of Subiaco, in the ecclesiastical territory. We were jolted along a rough ravine, through which the river Anio sped, and beetling mountains and shady trees, a distant convent and a picturesque cell on a hill, formed a view which so awoke the pictorial propensities of my friend, that he stopped the coupée (though we were assured that we should never reach our inn by nightfall, and that the road was dangerous in the dark), took out his portfolio, and began to sketch. As he drew, I continued to speak in support of an argument we had entered upon before. I had been complaining of the commonplace and ennui of life. Ashburn insisted that our existence was only too full of variety and change – tragic variety and wondrous incredible change. 'Even,' said the painter, 'as sky, and earth, and water seem for ever the same to the vulgar eye, and yet to the gifted one assume a thousand various guises and hues – now robed in purple – now shrouded in black – now resplendent with living gold – and anon sinking into sober and unobtrusive grey, so do our mortal lives change and vary. No living being among us but could tell a tale of soul-subduing joys and heart-consuming woes, worthy, had they their poet, of the imagination of Shakespeare or Goethe. The veriest weather-worn cabin is a study for colouring, and the meanest peasant will offer all the acts of a drama in the apparently dull routine of his humble life.'

'This is pure romance,' I replied; 'put it to the test. Let us take, for example, yonder woman descending the mountain-path.'

'What a figure!' cried Ashburn; 'oh that she would stay thus but one quarter of an hour! – she has come down to bathe her child – her upturned face – her dark hair – her picturesque costume – the little plump fellow bestriding her – the rude scenery around' –

'And the romantic tale she has to tell.'

'I would wager a louis that hers has been no common fate. She steps a goddess – her attitude, her looks, are all filled with majesty.'

I laughed at his enthusiasm, and accepted his bet. We hurried to join our fair peasantess, and thus formed acquaintance with Fanny Chaumont. A sudden storm, as we were engaged conversing with her, came, driven down from the tempest-bearing hills, and she gave us a cordial invitation to her cottage.

It was situated on a sunny, yet sheltered slope. There was a look of cheerfulness and '*aisance*' about it, beyond what is usually met in that part of Switzerland, reminding me of the cottages of the inhabitants of the free States. There, also, we found her husband. I always feel curious to know on whom a woman, who bears the stamp of superior intellect, who is beautiful and refined – for peasant as she was, Fanny was both – has been induced to bestow herself.

Louis Chaumont was considerably older than his wife; he was handsome, with brown lively eyes, curly chestnut hair, a visage embrowned by the sun, bearing every mark of having led an active, even an adventurous life; there was, besides, an expression which, if it were not ferocity, resembled it, in his vivacious glances, and in the sternness of his deeply-lined forehead; while she, in spite of her finely-formed brow, her majestic person, and her large expressive eyes, looked softness and patience itself. There was something incongruous in the pair, and more strangely matched they seemed when we heard their story. It lost me my louis, but proved Fanny at once to be a fitting heroine for romance, and was a lesson, moreover, to teach the strange pranks love can play with us, mingling fire and water, blending in one harmonious concord the harsh base and melodious tenor of two differently stringed instruments. Though their child was five years old, Fanny and her husband were attached to each other with the tenderness and passion of early love; they were happy – his faults were tempered by her angel disposition, and her too melancholy and feeling-fraught spirit was enlivened and made plastic to the purposes of this world by his energy and activity.

Fanny was a Bernese by birth: she was the child of humble cottagers, one among a large family. They lived on the brow of one summit and at the foot of another. The snowy mountains were piled about them; thaw-fed torrents brawled around; during the night a sound like thunder, a crash among the tempest-beaten pines would tell of an avalanche; or the snowdrift, whirring past the lattice, threatened to bury the little fabric. Winter was the season of peace in the deep vales, not so in the higher district. The peasant was often kept waking by the soft-falling snow which threatened insidiously to encroach on, and to overwhelm his habitation; or a straying cow would lead him far into the depths of the stormy hills, and his fearful family would count in agony the hours of his absence. Perpetual hardship and danger, however, rather brutify than exalt the soul of man; and those of the Swiss who are most deeply planted among the rocky wilds are often stultified and sullen.

Fanny opened her youthful eyes and observation on this scene. She was one of those lovely children whose beauty is heartfelt but indescribable: hers was the smooth candid brow, the large hazel eyes, half soft, half wild; the round dimpled cheek, the full sensitive mouth, the pointed chin, and (as framework to the picture) the luxuriant curly chestnut hair, and voice which is sweetest music. The exceeding beauty of little Fanny gained her the observation of the wife of the owner of the chateau which overlooked and commanded the district, and at ten years of age she became a frequent visitor there. Fanny's little soul was love, so she soon twined herself round the kind lady's heart, became a pet with her husband, and the favourite playmate of their only son.

One fête day Fanny had dined at the chateau. It had been fine warm spring weather, but wind and storm came on with the setting sun; the snow began to fall thickly, and it was decided that Fanny must pass the night in the chateau. She had been unusually eager to return home; and when the tempest came on, she crept near her protectress, and begged to be sent to her mother. '*C'est impossible*' – Fanny pressed no further, but she clambered to a window, and looked out wistfully to where, hidden by the hills, her parents' cottage stood. It was a fatal night for her: the thunders of frequent avalanches, the roaring of torrents, the crash of trees, spoke of devastation, and her home was its chief prey. Father, mother, brothers, and sisters, not one survived. Where, the day before, cottage and outhouse and flower garden had stood, the little lawn where she played, and the grove that sheltered her, there was now a monumental pile of snow, and the rocky path of a torrent; no trace remained, not one survivor to tell the tale. From that night Fanny became a constant inmate of the chateau.

It was Madame de Marville's project to give her a bourgeois education, which would raise her from the hardships of a peasant's life, and yet not elevate her above her natural position in society. She was brought up kindly, but humbly; it was the virtues of her disposition which raised her in the eyes of all around her – not any ill-judged favour of her benefactress. The night of the destruction of her family never passed away from her memory; it set a seal of untimely seriousness on her childish brow, awoke deep thoughts in her infant heart, and a strong resolve that while she lived, her beloved friends should find her, as far as her humble powers admitted, a source of good alone – a reason to rejoice that they had saved her from the destruction that had overwhelmed her family.

Thus Fanny grew up in beauty and in virtue. Her smiles were as the rainbows of her native torrents: her voice, her caresses, her light step, her unalterable sweetness and ceaseless devotion to the wishes of others, made her the idol of the family. Henry, the only child of her protectors, was of her own age, or but a few months her senior. Every time Henry returned from school to visit his parents, he found Fanny more beautiful, more kind, more attractive than before; and the first passion his youthful heart knew was for the lovely peasant girl, whose virtues sanctified his home. A look, a gesture betrayed his secret to his mother; she turned a hasty glance on Fanny, and saw on her countenance innocence and confidence alone. Half reassured, yet still fearful, Madame de Marville began to reflect on some cure for the threatened evil. She could not bear to send away Fanny; she was solicitous that her son should for the present reside in his home. The lovely girl was perfectly unconscious of the sentiments of the young seigneur; but would she always continue so? And was the burning heart that warmed her gentle bosom to be for ever insensible to the despotic and absorbing emotions of love?

It was with wonder, and a curious mixture of disappointed maternal pride and real gladness, that the lady at length discovered a passion dawning in fair Fanny's heart for Louis Chaumont, a peasant some ten years older than herself. It was natural that one with such high-wrought feelings as our heroine should love one to whom she could look up, and on whom to depend, rather than her childhood's playmate – the gay, thoughtless Henry. Louis's family had been the victim of a moral ruin, as hers of a physical one. They had been oppressed, reduced to poverty, driven from their homes by a feudal tyrant, and had come poor and forlorn from a distant district. His mother, accustomed to a bourgeois' life, died broken-hearted: his father, a man of violent passions, nourished in his own and in his son's heart, sentiments of hatred and revenge against the 'proud oppressors of the land.' They were obliged to labour hard, yet in the intervals of work, father and son would read or discourse concerning the ills attendant on humanity, and they traced all to the social system, which made the few the tyrants of the many.

Louis was handsome, bold, and active; he excelled his compeers in every hardy exercise; his resolution, his daring, made him, in spite of his poverty, a kind of leader among them. He had many faults; he was too full of passion, of the spirit of resistance and revenge; but his heart was kind; his understanding, when not thwarted, strong; and the very depth of his feelings made him keenly susceptible to love. Fanny, in her simple but majestic beauty, in her soft kindness of manner, mingled with the profoundest sensibility, made a deep impression on the young man's heart. His converse, so different and so superior to those of his fellows, won her attention.

Hitherto Fanny had never given utterance to the secrets of her soul. Habitual respect held her silent with Madame, and Henry, as spirited and as heedless as a chamois, could ill understand her; but Louis became the depository of the many feelings which, piled up in secrecy and silence, were half awful to herself; he brought reason, or what he deemed such, to direct her heart-born conclusions. To have heard them talk of life and death, and all its shows, you would have wondered by what freak philosophy had dressed herself in youth and a peasant's garb, and wandered from the schools to these untaught wilds.

Madame de Marville saw and encouraged this attachment. Louis was not exactly the person she would have selected for Fanny; but he was the only being for whom she had ever evinced a predilection; and, besides, the danger of a misalliance which threatened her own son, rendered her eager to build an insurmountable wall between him and the object of his affections. Thus Fanny enjoyed the heart-gladdening pride of hearing her choice applauded and praised by the person she most respected and loved in the world. As yet, however, love had been covert; the soul but not the apparent body of their intercourse. Louis was kept in awe by this high-minded girl, and Fanny had not yet learned her own secret. It was Henry who made the discovery for them; – Henry, who, with all the impetuosity of his vivacious character, contrived a thousand ways to come between them, who, stung by jealousy to injustice, reviled Louis for his ruin, his poverty, his opinions, and brought the spirit of dissension to disquiet a mind entirely bent, as she imagined, on holy and pure thoughts.

Under this clash of passion, the action of the drama rapidly developed itself, and, for nearly a year, a variety of scenes were acted among these secluded mountains of no interest save to the parties themselves, but to them fateful and engrossing. Louis and Fanny exchanged vows; but that sufficed not. Fanny insisted on the right of treating with uniform kindness the son of her best friend, in spite of his injustice and insolence. The young men were often, during the rural festivals, brought into angry collision. Fanny was the peacemaker: but a woman is the worst possible mediator between her rival lovers. Henry was sometimes irritated to complain to his father of Louis' presumption. The spirit of the French Revolution then awakening, rendered a peasant's assumptions peculiarly grating; and it required Madame de Marville's impartial gentleness to prevent Fanny's betrothed, as now he was almost considered, from being further oppressed.

At length it was decided that Henry should absent himself for a time, and visit Paris. He was enraged in the extreme by what he called his banishment. Noble and generous as he naturally was, love was the tyrant of his soul, and drove him almost to crime. He entered into a fierce quarrel with his rival on the very eve of his departure: it ended in a scene of violence and bloodshed. No great real harm was done; but Monsieur de Marville, hitherto scarcely kept back from such a measure by his wife, suddenly obtained an order for Louis (his father had died a year before) to quit the territory within twelve hours. Fanny was commanded, as she valued the favour of her friends, to give him up. The young men were both gone before any intercession could avail; and that kind of peace which resembles desolation took possession of the chateau.

Aware of the part she had taken in encouraging Fanny's attachment to her peasant-lover, Madame de Marville did not make herself a party to the tyranny of her husband; she requested only of her protégée to defer any decisive step, and not to quit her guardianship until the return of her son, which was to take place the following year. Fanny consented to such a delay, although in doing so she had to resist the angry representations of her lover, who exacted that she should quit the roof of his oppressors. It was galling to his proud spirit that she should continue to receive benefits from them, and injurious to his love that she should remain where his rival's name was the constant theme of discourse and the object of interest. Fanny in vain represented her debt of gratitude, the absence of Henry, the impossibility that she could feel any undue sentiment towards the young seigneur; not to hate him was a crime in Louis' eyes; yet how, in spite of his ill-conduct, could Fanny hate her childhood's playmate – her brother? His violent passions excited to their utmost height – jealousy and the sense of impotent indignation raging in his heart – Louis swore to revenge himself on the Marvilles – to forget and to abhor his mistress! – his last words were a malediction on them, and a violent denunciation of scorn upon her.

'It will all be well yet,' thought Fanny, as she strove to calm the tumultuous and painful emotions to which his intemperate passion gave rise. 'Not only are storms the birth of the wild elements, but of the heart of man, and we can oppose patience and fortitude alone to their destructive violence. A year will pass – I shall quit the chateau; Louis will acknowledge my truth, and retract his frightful words.'

She continued, therefore, to fulfil her duties cheerfully, not permitting her thoughts to dwell on the idea, that, in spite of her struggles, too painfully occupied her – the probability that Louis would in the end renounce or forget her; but committing her cause to the spirit of good, she trusted that its influence would in the end prevail.

She had, however, much to endure; for months passed, and no tidings reached her of Louis. Often she felt sick at heart; often she became the prey of the darkest despair; above all, her tender heart missed the fond attentions of love, the bliss of knowing that she bestowed happiness, and the unrestrained intercourse to which mutual affection had given rise. She cherished hope as a duty, and faith in love, rather than in her unjust and cruelly neglectful lover. It was a hard task, for she had nowhere to turn for consolation or encouragement. Madame de Marville marked with gladness the total separation between them. Now that the danger that threatened her son was averted, she relented having been influential in producing an attachment between Fanny and one whom she deemed unworthy of her. She redoubled her kindness, and, in the true Continental fashion, tried to get up a match between her and some one among her many and more prosperous admirers. She failed, but did not despair, till she saw the poor girl's cheek grow pale and her vivacity desert her, as month after month passed away, and the very name of Louis appeared to be forgotten by all except herself.

The stirring and terrible events that took place at this time in France added to Fanny's distress of mind. She had been familiarised to the discussion of the theories, now attempted to be put in practice, by the conversations of Chaumont. As each fresh account brought information of the guilty and sanguinary acts of men whose opinions were the same as those of her lover, her fears on his account increased. In a few words I shall hurry over this part of her story. Switzerland became agitated by the same commotions as tore the near kingdom. The peasantry rose in tumult; acts of violence and blood were committed; at first at a distance from her retired valley, but gradually approaching its precincts, until at last the tree of liberty was set up in the neighbouring village. Monsieur de Marville was an aristocrat of the most bigoted species. In vain was the danger represented to him, and the unwarlike state of his retinue. He armed them – he hurried down – he came unawares on the crowd who were proclaiming the triumph of liberty, rather by feasting than force. On the first attack, they were dispersed, and one or two among them were wounded; the pole they had gathered round was uprooted, the emblematic cap trampled to the earth. The governor returned victorious to his chateau.

This act of violence on his part seemed the match to fire a train of organised resistance to his authority, of which none had dreamt before. Strangers from other cantons thronged into the valley; rustic labours were cast aside; popular assemblies were held, and the peasants exercised in the use of arms. One was coming to place himself at their head, it was said, who had been a party in the tumults at Geneva. Louis Chaumont was coming – the champion of liberty, the sworn enemy of M. de Marville. The influence of his presence soon became manifest. The inhabitants of the chateau were besieged. If one ventured beyond a certain limit he was assailed. It was the resolve of Louis that all within its walls should surrender themselves to his mercy. What that might be, the proud curl of his lip and the fire that glanced from his dark eyes rendered scarcely problematic. Fanny would not believe the worst of her lover, but Monsieur and Madame de Marville, no longer restrained by any delicacy, spoke of the leveller in unmeasured terms of abhorrence, comparing him to the monsters who then reigned in France, while the danger they incurred through him added a bitter sting to their words. The peril grew each day; famine began to make its appearance in the chateau; while the intelligence which some of the more friendly peasants brought was indicative of preparations for a regular attack of the most formidable nature. A summons at last came from the insurgents. They were resolved to destroy the emblem of their slavery – the feudal halls of their tyrants. They declared their intention of firing the chateau the next day, and called on all within to deliver themselves up, if they would not be buried in its ruins. They offered their lives and free leave to depart to all, save the governor himself, who must place himself unconditionally at the mercy of their leader. 'The wretch,' exclaimed his lady, 'who thirsts for your blood! Fly! If there is yet time for flight; we, you see, are safe. Fly! Nor suffer these cruel dastards to boast of having murdered you.'

M. de Marville yielded to these entreaties and representations. He had sent for a military force to aid him – it had been denied. He saw that he himself, as the detested person, was the cause of danger to his family. It was therefore agreed that he should seek a chalet situated on a mountain ten leagues distant, where he might lie concealed till his family joined him. Accordingly, in a base disguise, he quitted at midnight the walls he was unable to defend; a miserable night for the unfortunate beings left behind. The coming day was to witness the destruction of their home; and they, beggars in the world, were to wander through the inhospitable mountains, till, with caution and terror, they could unobserved reach the remote and miserable chalet, and learn the fate of the unhappy fugitive. It was a sleepless night for all. To add to Madame's agony, she knew that her son's life was in danger in Paris – that he had been denounced – and, though yet untaken, his escape was still uncertain. From the turret of the castle that, situated high on a rock, commanded the valley below, she sat the livelong night watching for every sound – fearful of some shout, some report of firearms, which would announce the capture of her husband. It was September; the nights were chill; pale and trembling, she saw day break over the hills. Fanny had busied herself during these anxious hours by preparing for their departure; the terrified domestics had already fled; she, the lady, and the old lame gardener were all that remained. At dawn she brought forth the mule, and harnessed him to the rude vehicle which was to convey them to their place of refuge. Whatever was most valuable in the chateau had already been sent away long before, or was secreted; a few necessaries alone she provided. And now she ascended the turret stairs, and stood before her protectress, announcing that all was ready, and that they must depart. At this last moment, Madame de Marville appeared deprived of strength; she strove to rise – she sank to the ground in a fit. Forgetful of her deserted state, Fanny called aloud for help, and then her heart beat wildly as a quick, youthful step was heard on the stairs. Who could he be? Would 'he' come to insult their wretchedness – he, the author of their woe? The first glance changed the object of her terror. Henry flew to his mother's side, and, with broken exclamations and agitated questions, demanded an explanation of what he saw. He had fled for safety to the habitation of his parents – he found it deserted; the first voice he heard was that of Fanny crying for help – the first sight that presented itself was his mother, to all appearance dead, lying on the floor of the turret. Her recovery was followed by brief explanations, and a consultation of how his safety was to be provided for.

The name of Chaumont excited his bitterest execrations.

With a soldier's haughty resolve, he was darting from the castle to meet and to wreak vengeance on his rival. His mother threw herself at his feet, clasping his knees, calling wildly on him not to desert her. Fanny's gentle, sweet voice was of more avail to calm his passion. 'Chevalier,' she said, 'it is not thus that you must display your courage or protect the helpless. To encounter yonder infuriated mob would be to run on certain death; you must preserve yourself for your family – you must have pity on your mother, who cannot survive you. Be guided by me, I beseech you.'

Henry yielded to her voice, and a more reasonable arrangement took place. The departure of Madame de Marville and Fanny was expected at the village, and a pledge had been given that they should proceed unmolested. But deeply had the insurgents sworn that if the governor or his son (whose arrival in the chateau had been suspected) attempted to escape with them, they should be immediately sacrificed to 'justice'. No disguise would suffice – the active observation of their enemies was known. Every inhabitant of the castle had been numbered – the fate of each ascertained, save that of the two most detested – the governor, whose flight had not been discovered, and his son, whose arrival was so unexpected and ill-timed. As still they consulted, a beat to arms was heard in the valley below: it was the signal that the attack on the empty castle walls would soon begin. There was no time for delay or hesitation. Henry placed himself at the bottom of the charrette; straw and a variety of articles were heaped upon him; the two women ascended in trepidation; and the old gardener sat in front and held the reins.

In consequence of the disturbed state of the districts through which they were to pass, – where the appearance of one of the upper classes excited the fiercest enmity, and frightful insult, if not death, was their sure welcome, – Madame and her friend assumed a peasant's garb. And thus they wound their way down the steep; the unhappy lady weeping bitterly; Fanny, with tearless eyes, but with pale cheek and compressed lips, gazing for the last time on the abode which had been her refuge when, in helpless infancy, she was left an orphan – where kindness and benevolence had waited on her, and where her days had passed in innocence and peace. 'And he drives us away! – him, whom I loved – whom I love! – O misery!'

They reached the foot of the eminence on which the chateau was placed, and proceeded along the road which led directly through the village. With the approach of danger, vain regrets were exchanged for a lively sense of fear in the bosom of the hapless mother, and for the exertion of her courage and forethought in Fanny's more energetic mind. They passed a peasant or two, who uttered a malediction or imprecation on them as they went; then groups of two or three, who were even more violent in gesture and menace; when suddenly the sound of many steps came on their ears, and at a turn of the road they met Chaumont with a band of about twenty disciplined men.

'Fear not,' he said to Madame de Marville; 'I will protect you from danger till you are beyond the village.'

With a shriek, the lady, in answer, threw herself in Fanny's arms.

'Fear not, Madame – he dares not injure you. Begone, Louis! insult us not by your presence. Begone! I say.'

Fanny spoke angrily. She had not adopted this tone, but that the lady's terror, and the knowledge that even then the young soldier crouched at their feet, burnt to spring up and confront his enemy, made her use an authority which a woman always imagines that a lover dare not resist.

'I do not insult you,' repeated Chaumont – 'I save you. I have no quarrel with the lady; tyrants alone need fear me. You are not safe without my escort. Do not you, false girl, irritate me. I have ensured her escape; but yours – you are in my power.'

A violent movement at the bottom of the charrette called forth all Fanny's terrors.

'Take me!' she cried; 'do with me what you please; but you dare not, you cannot raise a finger against the innocent. Begone, I say! let me never see you more!'

'You are obeyed. On you fall the consequences.'

Thus, after many months of separation, did Fanny and her lover meet. She had purposed when she should see him to make an appeal to his better nature – his reason; she had meant to use her all-persuasive voice to recall him from the dangerous path he was treading. Several times, indeed, since his arrival in the valley, she had endeavoured to obtain an interview with him, but he dreaded her influence: he had resolved on revenge, and he feared to be turned back. But now the unexpected presence of his rival robbed her of her self-possession, and forced her to change her plans. She saw frightful danger in their meeting, and all her endeavours were directed to the getting rid of her lover.

Louis and his companions proceeded towards the chateau, while the charrette of the fugitives moved on in the opposite direction. They met many a ferocious group, who were rushing forward to aid in the destruction of their home; and glad they were, in that awful hour, that any object had power to divert the minds of their enemies from attention to themselves. The road they pursued wound through the valley; the precipitous mountain on one side, a brawling stream on the other.

Now they ascended higher and now again descended in their route, while the road, broken by the fall of rocks, intersected by torrents, which tore their way athwart it, made their progress slow. To get beyond the village was the aim of their desires; when, lo! just as they came upon it, and were in the very midst of its population, which was pouring towards the castle, suddenly the charrette sank in a deep rut; it half upset, and every spoke in the wheel giving way rendered the vehicle wholly useless.

Fanny had indeed already sprung to the ground to examine what hope remained: there was none. '*Grand Dieu*! we are lost!' were the first words that escaped her, while Madame stood aghast, trembling, almost insensible, knowing that the hope of her life, the existence of her son, depended on these miserable moments.

A peasant who owed Fanny some kindness now advanced, and in a kind of cavalier way, as if to blemish as much as he could the matter of his offer by its manner, told them, that, for the pleasure of getting rid of the aristocrats, he would lend his car – there it was, let them quickly bestow their lading in it and pursue their way. As he spoke, he caught up a box, and began the transfer from one car to the other.

'No, no!' cried Madame de Marville, as, with a scream, she sprang forward and grasped the arm of the man as he was in the very act of discovering her son's hiding-place. 'We will accept nothing from our base enemies! – Begone with your offers! we will die here, rather than accept anything from such "*canaille*".'

The word was electric. The fierce passions of the mob, excited by the mischief they were about to perpetrate, now burst like a stream into this new channel. With violent execrations they rushed upon the unfortunate woman: they would have torn her from the car, but already her son had sprung from his hiding-place, and, striking a violent blow at the foremost assailant, checked for a moment their brutal outrages. Then again, with a yell, such as the savage Indians alone could emulate, they rushed on their prey. Mother and son were torn asunder, and cries of '*À bas les aristocrats*!' – '*À la lanterne*!' declared too truly their sanguinary designs.

At this moment Louis appeared – Louis, whose fears for Fanny had overcome his indignation, and who returned to guard her; while she, perceiving him, with a burst of joy, called on him to rescue her friends. His cry of '*Arretez-vous*!' was loud and distinct amidst the uproar. It was obeyed; and then first he beheld his rival, his oppressor, his enemy in his power.

At first, rage inflamed every feature, to be replaced by an expression of triumph and implacable hatred. Fanny caught the fierce glance of his eye, and grew pale. She trembled as, trying to be calm, she said, 'Yes, you behold he is here. And you must save him – and your own soul. Rescue him from death, and be blest that your evil career enables you at least to perform this one good action.'

For a moment Louis seemed seeking for a word, as a man, meaning to stab, may fumble for his dagger's hilt, unable in his agitation to grasp his weapon.

'My friends,' at length he said, 'let the women depart – we have promised it. Ye may deal with the young aristocrat according to his merits.'

'*À la lanterne*!' burst in response from a hundred voices.

'Let his mother first depart!'

Could it be Louis that spoke these words, and had she loved this man? To appeal to him was to rouse a tiger from his lair. Another thought darted into Fanny's mind; she scarcely knew what she said or did: but already knives were drawn; already, with a thrill of horror, she thought she saw the blood of her childhood's playmate spilt like water on the earth. She rushed forward – she caught the upraised arm of one – 'He is no aristocrat!' she cried; 'he is my husband! – Will you murder one who, forgetting his birth, his duty, his honour, has married a peasant girl – one of yourselves?'

Even this appeal had little effect upon the mob; but it strangely affected her cruel lover. Grasping her arm with iron fingers, he cried, 'Is this tale true? Art thou married to that man – his wife?'

'Even so!' – the words died on her lips as she strove to form them, terrified by their purport, and the effect they might produce. An inexplicable expression passed over Chaumont's face; the fierceness that jealousy had engendered for a moment was exalted almost to madness, and then faded wholly away. The stony heart within him softened at once. A tide of warm, human, and overpowering emotion flowed into his soul: he looked on her he had loved, on her whom he had lost for ever; and tears rushed into his eyes, as he saw her trembling before him.

'Fear not,' at last he said; 'fear neither for him nor yourself. Poor girl! so young, you shall not lose all – so young, you shall not become a widow. He shall be saved!'

Yet it was no easy task, even for him, to stem the awakened passions of the bloodthirsty mob. He had spent many an hour in exciting them against their seigneurs, and now at once to control the violence to which he had given rise seemed impossible. Yet his energy, his strong will overcame all opposition. They should pierce the chevalier's heart, he swore, through his alone. He prevailed. He took the rein of their mule, and led them out of the village. All were silent; Fanny knew not what to say, and surprise held the others mute. Louis went with them until a turn in the road hid them from the view of the village. What his thoughts were, none could guess: he looked calm, as resigning the rein into the chevalier's hands, he gently bade them 'Farewell,' touching his hat in reply to their salutations. They moved on, and Fanny looked back to catch a last view of her lover: he was standing where they left him, when suddenly, instead of returning on his steps into the village, she saw him with rapid strides ascend the mountain-side, taking a well-known path that conducted him away from the scene of his late exploits. His pace was that of a man flying from pursuers – soon he was lost to sight.

Astonishment still kept the fugitives silent, as they pursued their way; and when at last joy broke forth, and Madame de Marville, rejoicing in their escape, embraced again and again her son, he with the softest tenderness thanked Fanny for his life: she answered not, but wept bitterly.

Late that night they reached the destined chalet, and found Monsieur de Marville arrived. It was a half-ruined miserable habitation perched among the snows, cold and bare; food was ill to be obtained, and danger breathed around them. Fanny attended on them with assiduous care, but she never spoke of the scene in the village; and though she strove to look the same, Henry never addressed her but she grew pale, and her voice trembled. She could not divine her absent lover's thoughts, but she knew that he believed her married to another; and that other, earnestly though she strove to rule her feelings, became an object of abhorrence to her.

Three weeks they passed in this wretched abode; three weeks replete with alarm, for the district around was in arms, and the life of Monsieur de Marville loudly threatened. They never slept but they dreaded the approach of the murderers; food they had little, and the inclement season visited them roughly. Fanny seemed to feel no inconvenience; her voice was cheerful: to console, encourage, and assist her friends appeared to occupy her whole heart. At length one night they were roused by a violent knocking at the door of their hut: Monsieur de Marville and Henry were on their feet in a moment, seizing their weapons as they rose. It was a domestic of their own, come to communicate the intelligence that the troubles were over, that the legal government had reasserted its authority, and invited the governor to return to Berne.

They descended from their mountain refuge, and the name of Louis hovered on Fanny's lips, but she spoke it not. He seemed everywhere forgotten. It was not until some time afterwards that she ascertained the fact that he had never been seen or heard of since he had parted from her on the morning of their escape. The villagers had waited for him in vain; they suspended their designs, for they all depended upon him; but he came not.

Monsieur and Madame de Marville returned to their chateau with their son, but Fanny remained behind. She would not inhabit the same roof as Henry; she recoiled even from receiving further benefits from his parents. What could she do? Louis would doubtless discover the falsehood of her marriage, but he dared not return; and even if he communicated with her, even though yet she loved him, could she unite herself with one accused too truly of the most frightful crimes? At first, these doubts agitated her, but by degrees they faded as oblivion closed over Chaumont's name; and he came not, and she heard not of him, and he was as dead to her. Then the memory of the past revived in her heart; her love awoke with her despair; his mysterious flight became the sole occupation of her thoughts; time rolled on and brought its changes. Madame de Marville died – Henry was united to another – Fanny remained, to her own thoughts, alone in the world. A relation, who lived at Subiaco, sent for her, and there she went to take up her abode. In vain she strove to wean herself from the memory of Louis – her love for him haunted her soul.

There was war in Europe, and every man was converted into a soldier; the country was thinned of its inhabitants, and each victory or defeat brought a new conscription. At length peace came again, and its return was celebrated with rejoicing. Many a soldier returned to his home – and one came back who had no home. A man, evidently suffering from recent wounds, wayworn and sick, asked for hospitality at Fanny's cottage; it was readily afforded, and he sat at her cottage fire, and removed his cap from his brow. His person was bent, his cheeks fallen in; yet those eyes of fire, that quick animated look, which almost brought the bright expression of youth back into his face, could never be forgotten. Fanny gazed almost in alarm, and then in joy, and at last, in her own sweet voice, she said, '*Et toi, Louis – tu aussi es de retour.*'

Louis had endured many a sorrow and many a hardship, and, most of all, he had been called on to wage battle with his own fierce spirit. The rage and hate which he had sedulously nourished suddenly became his tormentors and his tyrants – at the moment that love, before too closely allied to them, emancipated itself from their control. Love, which is the source of all that is most generous and noble in our nature, of self-devotion and of high intent, separated from the alloy he had blended with it, asserted its undivided power over him; strange that it should be so at the moment that he believed that he had lost her he loved for ever!

All his plans had been built for revenge. He would destroy the family that oppressed him; unbuild, stone by stone, the proud abode of their inheritance; he would be the sole refuge and support of his mistress in exile and in poverty. He had entered upon his criminal career with this design alone, and with the anticipation of ending all by heaping benefits and the gifts of fortune upon Fanny. The very steps he had taken, he now believed to be those that occasioned his defeat. He had lost her – the lovely and the good – he had lost her by proving unworthy, yet not so unworthy was he as to make her the victim of his crimes. The family he had vowed to ruin was now hers, and every injury that befell them visited her; to save her he must unweave his pernicious webs; to keep her scatheless, his dearest designs must fall to the ground.

A veil seemed rent before his eyes, he had fled, for he would not assist in the destruction of her fortunes; he had not returned, for it was torture to him to know that she lived, the wife of another. He entered the French army, but in every change his altered feelings pursued him, and to prove himself worthy of her he had lost was the constant aim of his ambition. His excellent conduct led to his promotion, and yet mishap still waited on him. He was wounded, even dangerously, and became so incapable of service as to be forced to solicit his dismission. This had occurred at the end of a hard campaign in Germany, and his intention was to pass into Italy, where a friend, with whom he had formed an intimacy in the army, promised to procure him some employment under Government. He passed through Subiaco in his way, and, ignorant of its occupiers, had asked for hospitality in his mistress's cottage.

If guilt can be expiated by repentance and reform, as is the best lesson of religion, Louis had expiated his. If constancy in love deserve reward, these lovers deserved that, which they reaped, in the happiness consequent on their union. Her image, side by side with all that is good in our nature, had dwelt in his heart, which thus became a shrine at which he sacrificed every evil passion. It was a greater bliss than he had ever dared to anticipate, to find, that in so doing, he had at the same time been conducing to the welfare of her he loved, and that the lost and idolised being whom he worshipped founded the happiness of her life upon his return to virtue, and the constancy of his affection.

Transformation

'Forthwith this frame of mine was wrench'd With a woful
 agony, Which forced me to begin my tale, And then it
 set me free.
'Since then, at an uncertain hour, That agony returns;
 And till my ghastly tale is told This heart within
 me burns.'
– Coleridge's *Ancient Mariner*

I have heard it said, that, when any strange, supernatural, and necromantic adventure has occurred to a human being, that being, however desirous he may be to conceal the same, feels at certain periods torn up as it were by an intellectual earthquake, and is forced to bare the inner depths of his spirit to another. I am a witness of the truth of this. I have dearly sworn to myself never to reveal to human ears the horrors to which I once, in excess of fiendly pride, delivered myself over. The holy man who heard my confession, and reconciled me to the Church, is dead. None knows that once –

Why should it not be thus? Why tell a tale of impious tempting of Providence, and soul-subduing humiliation? Why? answer me, ye who are wise in the secrets of human nature! I only know that so it is; and in spite of strong resolve, – of a pride that too much masters me – of shame, and even of fear, so to render myself odious to my species, – I must speak.

Genoa! my birthplace – proud city! looking upon the blue Mediterranean – dost thou remember me in my boyhood, when thy cliffs and promontories, thy bright sky and gay vineyards, were my world? Happy time! when to the young heart the narrow-bounded universe, which leaves, by its very limitation, free scope to the imagination, enchains our physical energies, and, sole period in our lives, innocence and enjoyment are united. Yet, who can look back to childhood, and not remember its sorrows and its harrowing fears? I was born with the most imperious, haughty, tameless spirit. I quailed before my father only; and he, generous and noble, but capricious and tyrannical, at once fostered and checked the wild impetuosity of my character, making obedience necessary, but inspiring no respect for the motives which guided his commands. To be a man, free, independent; or, in better words, insolent and domineering, was the hope and prayer of my rebel heart.

My father had one friend, a wealthy Genoese noble, who in a political tumult was suddenly sentenced to banishment, and his property confiscated. The Marchese Torella went into exile alone. Like my father, he was a widower: he had one child, the almost infant Juliet, who was left under my father's guardianship. I should certainly have been unkind to the lovely girl, but that I was forced by my position to become her protector. A variety of childish incidents all tended to one point, – to make Juliet see in me a rock of defence; I in her, one who must perish through the soft sensibility of her nature too rudely visited, but for my guardian care. We grew up together. The opening rose in May was not more sweet than this dear girl. An irradiation of beauty was spread over her face. Her form, her step, her voice – my heart weeps even now, to think of all of relying, gentle, loving, and pure, that she enshrined. When I was eleven and Juliet eight years of age, a cousin of mine, much older than either – he seemed to us a man – took great notice of my playmate; he called her his bride, and asked her to marry him. She refused, and he insisted, drawing her unwillingly towards him. With the countenance and emotions of a maniac I threw myself on him – I strove to draw his sword – I clung to his neck with the ferocious resolve to strangle him: he was obliged to call for assistance to disengage himself from me. On that night I led Juliet to the chapel of our house: I made her touch the sacred relics – I harrowed her child's heart, and profaned her child's lips with an oath, that she would be mine, and mine only.

Well, those days passed away. Torella returned in a few years, and became wealthier and more prosperous than ever. When I was seventeen, my father died; he had been magnificent to prodigality; Torella rejoiced that my minority would afford an opportunity for repairing my fortunes. Juliet and I had been affianced beside my father's deathbed – Torella was to be a second parent to me.

I desired to see the world, and I was indulged. I went to Florence, to Rome, to Naples; thence I passed to Toulon, and at length reached what had long been the bourne of my wishes, Paris. There was wild work in Paris then. The poor king, Charles the Sixth, now sane, now mad, now a monarch, now an abject slave, was the very mockery of humanity. The queen, the dauphin, the Duke of Burgundy, alternately friends and foes, – now meeting in prodigal feasts, now shedding blood in rivalry, – were blind to the miserable state of their country, and the dangers that impended over it, and gave themselves wholly up to dissolute enjoyment or savage strife. My character still followed me. I was arrogant and self-willed; I loved display, and above all, I threw off all control. My young friends were eager to foster passions which furnished them with pleasures. I was deemed handsome – I was master of every knightly accomplishment. I was disconnected with any political party. I grew a favourite with all: my presumption and arrogance was pardoned in one so young: I became a spoiled child. Who could control me? Not the letters and advice of Torella – only strong necessity visiting me in the abhorred shape of an empty purse. But there were means to refill this void. Acre after acre, estate after estate, I sold. My dress, my jewels, my horses and their caparisons, were almost unrivalled in gorgeous Paris, while the lands of my inheritance passed into possession of others.

The Duke of Orleans was waylaid and murdered by the Duke of Burgundy. Fear and terror possessed all Paris. The dauphin and the queen shut themselves up; every pleasure was suspended. I grew weary of this state of things, and my heart yearned for my boyhood's haunts. I was nearly a beggar, yet still I would go there, claim my bride, and rebuild my fortunes. A few happy ventures as a merchant would make me rich again. Nevertheless, I would not return in humble guise. My last act was to dispose of my remaining estate near Albaro for half its worth, for ready money. Then I despatched all kinds of artificers, arras, furniture of regal splendour, to fit up the last relic of my inheritance, my palace in Genoa. I lingered a little longer yet, ashamed at the part of the prodigal returned, which I feared I should play. I sent my horses. One matchless Spanish jennet I despatched to my promised bride: its caparisons flamed with jewels and cloth of gold. In every part I caused to be entwined the initials of Juliet and her Guido. My present found favour in hers and in her father's eyes.

Still to return a proclaimed spendthrift, the mark of impertinent wonder, perhaps of scorn, and to encounter singly the reproaches or taunts of my fellow-citizens, was no alluring prospect. As a shield between me and censure, I invited some few of the most reckless of my comrades to accompany me: thus I went armed against the world, hiding a rankling feeling, half fear and half penitence, by bravado.

I arrived in Genoa. I trod the pavement of my ancestral palace. My proud step was no interpreter of my heart, for I deeply felt that, though surrounded by every luxury, I was a beggar. The first step I took in claiming Juliet must widely declare me such. I read contempt or pity in the looks of all. I fancied that rich and poor, young and old, all regarded me with derision. Torella came not near me. No wonder that my second father should expect a son's deference from me in waiting first on him. But, galled and stung by a sense of my follies and demerit, I strove to throw the blame on others. We kept nightly orgies in Palazzo Carega. To sleepless, riotous nights followed listless, supine mornings. At the Ave Maria we showed our dainty persons in the streets, scoffing at the sober citizens, casting insolent glances on the shrinking women. Juliet was not among them – no, no; if she had been there, shame would have driven me away, if love had not brought me to her feet.

I grew tired of this. Suddenly I paid the Marchese a visit. He was at his villa, one among the many which deck the suburb of San Pietro d'Arena. It was the month of May, the blossoms of the fruit-trees were fading among thick, green foliage; the vines were shooting forth; the ground strewed with the fallen olive blooms; the firefly was in the myrtle hedge; heaven and earth wore a mantle of surpassing beauty. Torella welcomed me kindly, though seriously; and even his shade of displeasure soon wore away. Some resemblance to my father – some look and tone of youthful ingenuousness, softened the good old man's heart. He sent for his daughter – he presented me to her as her betrothed. The chamber became hallowed by a holy light as she entered. Hers was that cherub look, those large, soft eyes, full dimpled cheeks, and mouth of infantine sweetness, that expresses the rare union of happiness and love. Admiration first possessed me; she is mine! was the second proud emotion, and my lips curled with haughty triumph. I had not been the '*enfant gâté*' of the beauties of France not to have learnt the art of pleasing the soft heart of woman. If towards men I was overbearing, the deference I paid to them was the more in contrast. I commenced my courtship by the display of a thousand gallantries to Juliet, who, vowed to me from infancy, had never admitted the devotion of others; and who, though accustomed to expressions of admiration, was uninitiated in the language of lovers.

For a few days all went well. Torella never alluded to my extravagance; he treated me as a favourite son. But the time came, as we discussed the preliminaries to my union with his daughter, when this fair face of things should be overcast. A contract had been drawn up in my father's lifetime. I had rendered this, in fact, void by having squandered the whole of the wealth which was to have been shared by Juliet and myself. Torella, in consequence, chose to consider this bond as cancelled, and proposed another, in which, though the wealth he bestowed was immeasurably increased, there were so many restrictions as to the mode of spending it, that I, who saw independence only in free career being given to my own imperious will, taunted him as taking advantage of my situation, and refused utterly to subscribe to his conditions. The old man mildly strove to recall me to reason. Roused pride became the tyrant of my thought: I listened with indignation – I repelled him with disdain.

'Juliet, thou art mine! Did we not interchange vows in our innocent childhood? Are we not one in the sight of God? and shall thy cold-hearted, cold-blooded father divide us?

Be generous, my love, be just; take not away a gift, last treasure of thy Guido – retract not thy vows – let us defy the world, and, setting at nought the calculations of age, find in our mutual affection a refuge from every ill.'

Fiend I must have been with such sophistry to endeavour to poison that sanctuary of holy thought and tender love. Juliet shrank from me affrighted. Her father was the best and kindest of men, and she strove to show me how, in obeying him, every good would follow. He would receive my tardy submission with warm affection, and generous pardon would follow my repentance; – profitless words for a young and gentle daughter to use to a man accustomed to make his will law, and to feel in his own heart a despot so terrible and stern that he could yield obedience to nought save his own imperious desires! My resentment grew with resistance; my wild companions were ready to add fuel to the flame. We laid a plan to carry off Juliet. At first it appeared to be crowned with success. Midway, on our return, we were overtaken by the agonised father and his attendants. A conflict ensued. Before the city guard came to decide the victory in favour of our antagonists, two of Torella's servitors were dangerously wounded.

This portion of my history weighs most heavily with me. Changed man as I am, I abhor myself in the recollection. May none who hear this tale ever have felt as I. A horse driven to fury by a rider armed with barbed spurs was not more a slave than I to the violent tyranny of my temper. A fiend possessed my soul, irritating it to madness. I felt the voice of conscience within me;

but if I yielded to it for a brief interval, it was only to be a moment after torn, as by a whirlwind, away – borne along on the stream of desperate rage – the plaything of the storms engendered by pride. I was imprisoned, and, at the instance of Torella, set free. Again I returned to carry off both him and his child to France, which hapless country, then preyed on by freebooters and gangs of lawless soldiery, offered a grateful refuge to a criminal like me. Our plots were discovered. I was sentenced to banishment; and, as my debts were already enormous, my remaining property was put in the hands of commissioners for their payment. Torella again offered his mediation, requiring only my promise not to renew my abortive attempts on himself and his daughter. I spurned his offers, and fancied that I triumphed when I was thrust out from Genoa, a solitary and penniless exile. My companions were gone: they had been dismissed the city some weeks before, and were already in France. I was alone – friendless, with neither sword at my side, nor ducat in my purse.

I wandered along the sea-shore, a whirlwind of passion possessing and tearing my soul. It was as if a live coal had been set burning in my breast. At first I meditated on what 'I should do'. I would join a band of freebooters. Revenge! – the word seemed balm to me; I hugged it, caressed it, till, like a serpent, it stung me. Then again I would abjure and despise Genoa, that little corner of the world. I would return to Paris, where so many of my friends swarmed; where my services would be eagerly accepted; where I would carve out fortune with my sword, and make my paltry birthplace and the false Torella rue the day when they drove me, a new Coriolanus, from her walls. I would return to Paris – thus on foot – a beggar – and present myself in my poverty to those I had formerly entertained sumptuously? There was gall in the mere thought of it.

The reality of things began to dawn upon my mind, bringing despair in its train. For several months I had been a prisoner: the evils of my dungeon had whipped my soul to madness, but they had subdued my corporeal frame. I was weak and wan. Torella had used a thousand artifices to administer to my comfort; I had detected and scorned them all, and I reaped the harvest of my obduracy. What was to be done? Should I crouch before my foe, and sue for forgiveness? – Die rather ten thousand deaths! – Never should they obtain that victory! Hate – I swore eternal hate! Hate from whom? – to whom? – From a wandering outcast – to a mighty noble! I and my feelings were nothing to them: already had they forgotten one so unworthy. And Juliet! – her angel face and sylph-like form gleamed among the clouds of my despair with vain beauty; for I had lost her – the glory and flower of the world! Another will call her his! – that smile of paradise will bless another!

Even now my heart fails within me when I recur to this rout of grim-visaged ideas. Now subdued almost to tears, now raving in my agony, still I wandered along the rocky shore, which grew at each step wilder and more desolate. Hanging rocks and hoar precipices overlooked the tideless ocean; black caverns yawned; and for ever, among the seaworn recesses, murmured and dashed the unfruitful waters. Now my way was almost barred by an abrupt promontory, now rendered nearly impracticable by fragments fallen from the cliff. Evening was at hand, when, seaward, arose, as if on the waving of a wizard's wand, a murky web of clouds, blotting the late azure sky, and darkening and disturbing the till now placid deep. The clouds had strange, fantastic shapes, and they changed and mingled and seemed to be driven about by a mighty spell. The waves raised their white crests; the thunder first muttered, then roared from across the waste of waters, which took a deep purple dye, flecked with foam.

The spot where I stood looked, on one side, to the widespread ocean; on the other, it was barred by a rugged promontory. Round this cape suddenly came, driven by the wind, a vessel. In vain the mariners tried to force a path for her to the open sea – the gale drove her on the rocks. It will perish! – all on board will perish! Would I were among them! And to my young heart the idea of death came for the first time blended with that of joy. It was an awful sight to behold that vessel struggling with her fate. Hardly could I discern the sailors, but I heard them. It was soon all over! A rock, just covered by the tossing waves, and so unperceived, lay in wait for its prey. A crash of thunder broke over my head at the moment that, with a frightful shock, the vessel dashed upon her unseen enemy.

In a brief space of time she went to pieces. There I stood in safety; and there were my fellow-creatures battling, how hopelessly, with annihilation. Methought I saw them struggling – too truly did I hear their shrieks, conquering the barking surges in their shrill agony. The dark breakers threw hither and thither the fragments of the wreck: soon it disappeared. I had been fascinated to gaze till the end: at last I sank on my knees – I covered my face with my hands. I again looked up; something was floating on the billows towards the shore. It neared and neared. Was that a human form? It grew more and more distinct; and at last a mighty wave, lifting the whole freight, lodged it upon a rock.

A human being bestriding a sea-chest! – a human being! Yet was it one? Surely never such had existed before – a misshapen dwarf, with squinting eyes, distorted features, and body deformed, till it became a horror to behold. My blood, lately warming towards a fellow-being so snatched from a watery tomb, froze in my heart. The dwarf got off his chest; he tossed his straight, struggling hair from his odious visage.

'By St. Beelzebub!' he exclaimed, 'I have been well bested.' He looked round and saw me. 'Oh, by the fiend! Here is another ally of the mighty One. To what saint did you offer prayers, friend – if not to mine? Yet I remember you not on board.'

I shrank from the monster and his blasphemy. Again he questioned me, and I muttered some inaudible reply. He continued: –

'Your voice is drowned by this dissonant roar. What a noise the big ocean makes! Schoolboys bursting from their prison are not louder than these waves set free to play. They disturb me. I will no more of their ill-timed brawling. Silence, hoary One! – Winds, avaunt! – to your homes! – Clouds, fly to the antipodes, and leave our heaven clear!'

As he spoke, he stretched out his two long, lank arms, that looked like spider's claws, and seemed to embrace with them the expanse before him. Was it a miracle? The clouds became broken and fled; the azure sky first peeped out, and then was spread a calm field of blue above us; the stormy gale was exchanged to the softly breathing west; the sea grew calm; the waves dwindled to riplets.

'I like obedience even in these stupid elements,' said the dwarf. 'How much more in the tameless mind of man! It was a well-got-up storm, you must allow – and all of my own making.'

It was tempting Providence to interchange talk with this magician. But 'Power', in all its shapes, is respected by man. Awe, curiosity, a clinging fascination, drew me towards him.

'Come, don't be frightened, friend,' said the wretch: 'I am good-humoured when pleased; and something does please me in your well-proportioned body and handsome face, though you look a little woe-begone. You have suffered a land – I, a sea wreck. Perhaps I can allay the tempest of your fortunes as I did my own. Shall we be friends?' – And he held out his hand; I could not touch it. 'Well, then, companions – that will do as well. And now, while I rest after the buffeting I underwent just now, tell me why, young and gallant as you seem, you wander thus alone and downcast on this wild sea-shore.'

The voice of the wretch was screeching and horrid, and his contortions as he spoke were frightful to behold. Yet he did gain a kind of influence over me, which I could not master, and I told him my tale. When it was ended, he laughed long and loud: the rocks echoed back the sound: hell seemed yelling around me.

'Oh, thou cousin of Lucifer!' said he; 'so thou too hast fallen through thy pride; and, though bright as the son of Morning, thou art ready to give up thy good looks, thy bride, and thy well-being, rather than submit thee to the tyranny of good. I honour thy choice, by my soul! – So thou hast fled, and yield the day; and mean to starve on these rocks, and to let the birds peck out thy dead eyes, while thy enemy and thy betrothed rejoice in thy ruin. Thy pride is strangely akin to humility, methinks.'

As he spoke, a thousand fanged thoughts stung me to the heart.

'What would you that I should do?' I cried.

'I! – Oh, nothing, but lie down and say your prayers before you die. But, were I you, I know the deed that should be done.'

I drew near him. His supernatural powers made him an oracle in my eyes; yet a strange unearthly thrill quivered through my frame as I said,

'Speak! – teach me – what act do you advise?'

'Revenge thyself, man! – humble thy enemies! – set thy foot on the old man's neck, and possess thyself of his daughter!'

'To the east and west I turn,' cried I, 'and see no means! Had I gold, much could I achieve; but, poor and single, I am powerless.'

The dwarf had been seated on his chest as he listened to my story. Now he got off; he touched a spring; it flew open! What a mine of wealth – of blazing jewels, beaming gold, and pale silver – was displayed therein. A mad desire to possess this treasure was born within me.

'Doubtless,' I said, 'one so powerful as you could do all things.'

'Nay,' said the monster humbly, 'I am less omnipotent than I seem. Some things I possess which you may covet; but I would give them all for a small share, or even for a loan of what is yours.'

'My possessions are at your service,' I replied bitterly – 'my poverty, my exile, my disgrace – I make a free gift of them all.'

'Good! I thank you. Add one other thing to your gift, and my treasure is yours.'

'As nothing is my sole inheritance, what besides nothing would you have?'

'Your comely face and well-made limbs.'

I shivered. Would this all-powerful monster murder me? I had no dagger. I forgot to pray – but I grew pale.

'I ask for a loan, not a gift,' said the frightful thing: 'lend me your body for three days – you shall have mine to cage your soul the while, and, in payment, my chest. What say you to the bargain? – Three short days.'

We are told that it is dangerous to hold unlawful talk; and well do I prove the same. Tamely written down, it may seem incredible that I should lend any ear to this proposition; but, in spite of his unnatural ugliness, there was something fascinating in a being whose voice could govern earth, air, and sea. I felt a keen desire to comply; for with that chest I could command the worlds. My only hesitation resulted from a fear that he would not be true to his bargain. Then, I thought, I shall soon die here on these lonely sands, and the limbs he covets will be mine no more: – it is worth the chance. And, besides, I knew that, by all the rules of art-magic, there were formula and oaths which none of its practisers dared break. I hesitated to reply; and he went on, now displaying his wealth, now speaking of the petty price he demanded, till it seemed madness to refuse. Thus is it; – place our bark in the current of the stream, and down, over fall and cataract it is hurried; give up our conduct to the wild torrent of passion, and we are away, we know not whither.

He swore many an oath, and I adjured him by many a sacred name; till I saw this wonder of power, this ruler of the elements, shiver like an autumn leaf before my words; and as if the spirit spake unwillingly and perforce within him, at last, he, with broken voice, revealed the spell whereby he might be obliged, did he wish to play me false, to render up the unlawful spoil. Our warm life-blood must mingle to make and to mar the charm.

Enough of this unholy theme. I was persuaded – the thing was done. The morrow dawned upon me as I lay upon the shingles, and I knew not my own shadow as it fell from me. I felt myself changed to a shape of horror, and cursed my easy faith and blind credulity. The chest was there – there the gold and precious stones for which I had sold the frame of flesh which nature had given me. The sight a little stilled my emotions: three days would soon be gone.

They did pass. The dwarf had supplied me with a plenteous store of food. At first I could hardly walk, so strange and out of joint were all my limbs; and my voice – it was that of the fiend. But I kept silent, and turned my face to the sun, that I might not see my shadow, and counted the hours, and ruminated on my future conduct. To bring Torella to my feet – to possess my Juliet in spite of him – all this my wealth could easily achieve. During dark night I slept, and dreamt of the accomplishment of my desires. Two suns had set – the third dawned. I was agitated, fearful. Oh expectation, what a frightful thing art thou, when kindled more by fear than hope! How dost thou twist thyself round the heart, torturing its pulsations! How dost thou dart unknown pangs all through our feeble mechanism, now seeming to shiver us like broken glass, to nothingness – now giving us a fresh strength, which can 'do' nothing, and so torments us by a sensation, such as the strong man must feel who cannot break his fetters, though they bend in his grasp. Slowly paced the bright, bright orb up the eastern sky; long it lingered in the zenith, and still more slowly wandered down the west: it touched the horizon's verge – it was lost! Its glories were on the summits of the cliff – they grew dun and grey. The evening star shone bright. He will soon be here.

He came not! – By the living heavens, he came not! And night dragged out its weary length, and, in its decaying age, 'day began to grizzle its dark hair;' and the sun rose again on the most miserable wretch that ever upbraided its light. Three days thus I passed. The jewels and the gold – oh, how I abhorred them!

Well, well – I will not blacken these pages with demoniac ravings. All too terrible were the thoughts, the raging tumult of ideas that filled my soul. At the end of that time I slept; I had not before since the third sunset; and I dreamt that I was at

Juliet's feet, and she smiled, and then she shrieked – for she saw my transformation – and again she smiled, for still her beautiful lover knelt before her. But it was not I – it was he, the fiend, arrayed in my limbs, speaking with my voice, winning her with my looks of love. I strove to warn her, but my tongue refused its office; I strove to tear him from her, but I was rooted to the ground – I awoke with the agony. There were the solitary hoar precipices – there the plashing sea, the quiet strand, and the blue sky over all. What did it mean? Was my dream but a mirror of the truth? Was he wooing and winning my betrothed? I would on the instant back to Genoa – but I was banished. I laughed – the dwarf's yell burst from my lips – 'I' banished! Oh no! they had not exiled the foul limbs I wore; I might with these enter, without fear of incurring the threatened penalty of death, my own, my native city.

I began to walk towards Genoa. I was somewhat accustomed to my distorted limbs; none were ever so ill-adapted for a straightforward movement; it was with infinite difficulty that I proceeded. Then, too, I desired to avoid all the hamlets strewed here and there on the sea-beach, for I was unwilling to make a display of my hideousness. I was not quite sure that, if seen, the mere boys would not stone me to death as I passed, for a monster; some ungentle salutations I did receive from the few peasants or fishermen I chanced to meet. But it was dark night before I approached Genoa. The weather was so balmy and sweet that it struck me that the Marchese and his daughter would very probably have quitted the city for their country retreat. It was from Villa Torella that I had attempted to carry off Juliet; I had spent many an hour reconnoitring the spot, and knew each inch of ground in its vicinity. It was beautifully situated, embosomed in trees, on the margin of a stream. As I drew near, it became evident that my conjecture was right; nay, moreover, that the hours were being then devoted to feasting and merriment. For the house was lighted up; strains of soft and gay music were wafted towards me by the breeze. My heart sank within me. Such was the generous kindness of Torella's heart that I felt sure that he would not have indulged in public manifestations of rejoicing just after my unfortunate banishment, but for a cause I dared not dwell upon.

The country people were all alive and flocking about; it became necessary that I should conceal myself; and yet I longed to address some one, or to hear others discourse, or in any way to gain intelligence of what was really going on. At length, entering the walks that were in immediate vicinity to the mansion, I found one dark enough to veil my excessive frightfulness; and yet others as well as I were loitering in its shade. I soon gathered all I wanted to know – all that first made my very heart die with horror, and then boil with indignation. To-morrow Juliet was to be given to the penitent, reformed, beloved Guido – to-morrow my bride was to pledge her vows to a fiend from hell! And I did this! – my accursed pride – my demoniac violence and wicked self-idolatry had caused this act. For if I had acted as the wretch who had stolen my form had acted – if, with a mien at once yielding and dignified, I had presented myself to Torella, saying, I have done wrong, forgive me; I am unworthy of your angel-child, but permit me to claim her hereafter, when my altered conduct shall manifest that I abjure my vices, and endeavour to become in some sort worthy of her. I go to serve against the infidels; and when my zeal for religion and my true penitence for the past shall appear to you to cancel my crimes, permit me again to call myself your son. Thus had he spoken; and the penitent was welcomed even as the prodigal son of Scripture: the fatted calf was killed for him; and he, still pursuing the same path, displayed such open-hearted regret for his follies, so humble a concession of all his rights, and so ardent a resolve to reacquire them by a life of contrition and virtue, that he quickly conquered the kind old man; and full pardon, and the gift of his lovely child, followed in swift succession.

Oh, had an angel from Paradise whispered to me to act thus! But now, what would be the innocent Juliet's fate? Would God permit the foul union – or, some prodigy destroying it, link the dishonoured name of Carega with the worst of crimes? To-morrow at dawn they were to be married: there was but one way to prevent this – to meet mine enemy, and to enforce the ratification of our agreement. I felt that this could only be done by a mortal struggle. I had no sword – if indeed my distorted arms could wield a soldier's weapon – but I had a dagger, and in that lay my hope. There was no time for pondering or balancing nicely the question: I might die in the attempt; but besides the burning jealousy and despair of my own heart, honour, mere humanity, demanded that I should fall rather than not destroy the machinations of the fiend.

The guests departed – the lights began to disappear; it was evident that the inhabitants of the villa were seeking repose. I hid myself among the trees – the garden grew desert – the gates were closed – I wandered round and came under a window – ah! well did I know the same! – a soft twilight glimmered in the room – the curtains were half withdrawn. It was the temple of innocence and beauty. Its magnificence was tempered, as it were, by the slight disarrangements occasioned by its being dwelt in, and all the objects scattered around displayed the taste of her who hallowed it by her presence. I saw her enter with a quick light step – I saw her approach the window – she drew back the curtain yet further, and looked out into the night. Its breezy freshness played among her ringlets, and wafted them from the transparent marble of her brow. She clasped her hands, she raised her eyes to heaven. I heard her voice. Guido! she softly murmured – mine own Guido! and then, as if overcome by the fulness of her own heart, she sank on her knees; – her upraised eyes – her graceful attitude – the beaming thankfulness that lighted up her face – oh, these are tame words! Heart of mine, thou imagest ever, though thou canst not portray, the celestial beauty of that child of light and love.

I heard a step – a quick firm step along the shady avenue. Soon I saw a cavalier, richly dressed, young and, methought, graceful to look on, advance. I hid myself yet closer. The youth approached; he paused beneath the window. She arose, and again looking out she saw him, and said – I cannot, no, at this distant time I cannot record her terms of soft silver tenderness; to me they were spoken, but they were replied to by him.

'I will not go,' he cried: 'here where you have been, where your memory glides like some heaven-visiting ghost, I will pass the long hours till we meet, never, my Juliet, again, day or night, to part. But do thou, my love, retire; the cold morn and fitful breeze will make thy cheek pale, and fill with languor thy love-lighted eyes. Ah, sweetest! Could I press one kiss upon them, I could, methinks, repose.'

And then he approached still nearer, and methought he was about to clamber into her chamber. I had hesitated, not to terrify her; now I was no longer master of myself. I rushed forward – I threw myself on him – I tore him away – I cried, 'O loathsome and foul-shaped wretch!'

I need not repeat epithets, all tending, as it appeared, to rail at a person I at present feel some partiality for. A shriek rose from Juliet's lips. I neither heard nor saw – I 'felt' only mine enemy, whose throat I grasped, and my dagger's hilt; he struggled, but could not escape. At length hoarsely he breathed these words: 'Do! – strike home! Destroy this body – you will still live: may your life be long and merry!'

The descending dagger was arrested at the word, and he, feeling my hold relax, extricated himself and drew his sword, while the uproar in the house, and flying of torches from one room to the other, showed that soon we should be separated. In the midst of my frenzy there was much calculation:

– fall I might, and so that he did not survive, I cared not for the death-blow I might deal against myself. While still, therefore, he thought I paused, and while I saw the villanous resolve to take advantage of my hesitation, in the sudden thrust he made at me, I threw myself on his sword, and at the same moment plunged my dagger, with a true, desperate aim, in his side. We fell together, rolling over each other, and the tide of blood that flowed from the gaping wound of each mingled on the grass. More I know not – I fainted.

Again I return to life: weak almost to death, I found myself stretched upon a bed – Juliet was kneeling beside it. Strange! My first broken request was for a mirror. I was so wan and ghastly, that my poor girl hesitated, as she told me afterwards; but, by the mass! I thought myself a right proper youth when I saw the dear reflection of my own well-known features. I confess it is a weakness, but I avow it, I do entertain a considerable affection for the countenance and limbs I behold, whenever I look at a glass; and have more mirrors in my house, and consult them oftener, than any beauty in Genoa. Before you too much condemn me, permit me to say that no one better knows than I the value of his own body; no one, probably, except myself, ever having had it stolen from him.

Incoherently I at first talked of the dwarf and his crimes, and reproached Juliet for her too easy admission of his love. She thought me raving, as well she might; and yet it was some time before I could prevail on myself to admit that the Guido whose penitence had won her back for me was myself; and while

I cursed bitterly the monstrous dwarf, and blest the well-directed blow that had deprived him of life, I suddenly checked myself when I heard her say, Amen! Knowing that him whom she reviled was my very self. A little reflection taught me silence – a little practice enabled me to speak of that frightful night without any very excessive blunder. The wound I had given myself was no mockery of one – it was long before I recovered – and as the benevolent and generous Torella sat beside me, talking such wisdom as might win friends to repentance, and mine own dear Juliet hovered near me, administering to my wants, and cheering me by her smiles, the work of my bodily cure and mental reform went on together. I have never, indeed, wholly recovered my strength – my cheek is paler since – my person a little bent. Juliet sometimes ventures to allude bitterly to the malice that caused this change, but I kiss her on the moment, and tell her all is for the best. I am a fonder and more faithful husband, and true is this – but for that wound, never had I called her mine.

I did not revisit the sea-shore, nor seek for the fiend's treasure; yet, while I ponder on the past, I often think, and my confessor was not backward in favouring the idea, that it might be a good rather than an evil spirit, sent by my guardian angel, to show me the folly and misery of pride. So well at least did I learn this lesson, roughly taught as I was, that I am known now by all my friends and fellow-citizens by the name of Guido il Cortese.

The Mortal Immortal

July 16, 1833. – This is a memorable anniversary for me; on it I complete my three hundred and twenty-third year!

The Wandering Jew? – certainly not. More than eighteen centuries have passed over his head. In comparison with him, I am a very young Immortal.

Am I, then, immortal? This is a question which I have asked myself, by day and night, for now three hundred and three years, and yet cannot answer it. I detected a grey hair amidst my brown locks this very day – that surely signifies decay. Yet it may have remained concealed there for three hundred years – for some persons have become entirely white-headed before twenty years of age.

I will tell my story, and my reader shall judge for me. I will tell my story, and so contrive to pass some few hours of a long eternity, become so wearisome to me. For ever! Can it be? to live for ever! I have heard of enchantments, in which the victims were plunged into a deep sleep, to wake, after a hundred years, as fresh as ever: I have heard of the Seven Sleepers

– thus to be immortal would not be so burthensome: but, oh! the weight of never-ending time – the tedious passage of the still-succeeding hours! How happy was the fabled Nourjahad! – But to my task.

All the world has heard of Cornelius Agrippa. His memory is as immortal as his arts have made me. All the world has also heard of his scholar, who, unawares, raised the foul fiend during his master's absence, and was destroyed by him. The report, true or false, of this accident, was attended with many inconveniences to the renowned philosopher. All his scholars at once deserted him – his servants disappeared. He had no one near him to put coals on his ever-burning fires while he slept, or to attend to the changeful colours of his medicines while he studied. Experiment after experiment failed, because one pair of hands was insufficient to complete them: the dark spirits laughed at him for not being able to retain a single mortal in his service.

I was then very young – very poor – and very much in love. I had been for about a year the pupil of Cornelius, though I was absent when this accident took place. On my return, my friends implored me not to return to the alchymist's abode. I trembled as I listened to the dire tale they told; I required no second warning; and when Cornelius came and offered me a purse of gold if I would remain under his roof, I felt as if Satan himself tempted me. My teeth chattered – my hair stood on end; – I ran off as fast as my trembling knees would permit.

My failing steps were directed whither for two years they had every evening been attracted, – a gently bubbling spring of pure living water, beside which lingered a dark-haired girl, whose beaming eyes were fixed on the path I was accustomed each night to tread. I cannot remember the hour when I did not love Bertha; we had been neighbours and playmates from infancy, – her parents, like mine, were of humble life, yet respectable, – our attachment had been a source of pleasure to them. In an evil hour, a malignant fever carried off both her father and mother, and Bertha became an orphan. She would have found a home beneath my paternal roof, but, unfortunately, the old lady of the near castle, rich, childless, and solitary, declared her intention to adopt her. Henceforth Bertha was clad in silk – inhabited a marble palace – and was looked on as being highly favoured by fortune. But in her new situation among her new associates, Bertha remained true to the friend of her humbler days; she often visited the cottage of my father, and when forbidden to go thither, she would stray towards the neighbouring wood, and meet me beside its shady fountain.

She often declared that she owed no duty to her new protectress equal in sanctity to that which bound us. Yet still I was too poor to marry, and she grew weary of being tormented on my account. She had a haughty but an impatient spirit, and grew angry at the obstacles that prevented our union. We met now after an absence, and she had been sorely beset while I was away; she complained bitterly, and almost reproached me for being poor. I replied hastily, –

'I am honest, if I am poor! – were I not, I might soon become rich!'

This exclamation produced a thousand questions. I feared to shock her by owning the truth, but she drew it from me; and then, casting a look of disdain on me, she said –

'You pretend to love, and you fear to face the Devil for my sake!'

I protested that I had only dreaded to offend her; – while she dwelt on the magnitude of the reward that I should receive. Thus encouraged – shamed by her – led on by love and hope, laughing at my late fears, with quick steps and a light heart, I returned to accept the offers of the alchymist, and was instantly installed in my office.

A year passed away. I became possessed of no insignificant sum of money. Custom had banished my fears. In spite of the most painful vigilance, I had never detected the trace of a cloven foot; nor was the studious silence of our abode ever disturbed by demoniac howls. I still continued my stolen interviews with Bertha, and Hope dawned on me – Hope – but not perfect joy; for Bertha fancied that love and security were enemies, and her pleasure was to divide them in my bosom. Though true of heart, she was somewhat of a coquette in manner; and I was jealous as a Turk. She slighted me in a thousand ways, yet would never acknowledge herself to be in the wrong. She would drive me mad with anger, and then force me to beg her pardon. Sometimes she fancied that I was not sufficiently submissive, and then she had some story of a rival, favoured by her protectress. She was surrounded by silk-clad youths – the rich and gay. What chance had the sad-robed scholar of Cornelius compared with these?

On one occasion, the philosopher made such large demands upon my time, that I was unable to meet her as I was wont. He was engaged in some mighty work, and I was forced to remain, day and night, feeding his furnaces and watching his chemical preparations. Bertha waited for me in vain at the fountain. Her haughty spirit fired at this neglect; and when at last I stole out during the few short minutes allotted to me for slumber, and hoped to be consoled by her, she received me with disdain, dismissed me in scorn, and vowed that any man should possess her hand rather than he who could not be in two places at once for her sake. She would be revenged! And truly she was. In my dingy retreat I heard that she had been hunting, attended by Albert Hoffer. Albert Hoffer was favoured by her protectress; and the three passed in cavalcade before my smoky window. Methought that they mentioned my name; it was followed by a laugh of derision, as her dark eyes glanced contemptuously towards my abode.

Jealousy, with all its venom and all its misery, entered my breast. Now I shed a torrent of tears, to think that I should never call her mine; and, anon, I imprecated a thousand curses on her inconstancy. Yet, still I must stir the fires of the alchymist, still attend on the changes of his unintelligible medicines.

Cornelius had watched for three days and nights, nor closed his eyes. The progress of his alembics was slower than he expected: in spite of his anxiety, sleep weighed upon his eyelids. Again and again he threw off drowsiness with more than human energy; again and again it stole away his senses. He eyed his crucibles wistfully. 'Not ready yet,' he murmured; 'will another night pass before the work is accomplished? Winzy, you are vigilant – you are faithful – you have slept, my boy – you slept last night. Look at that glass vessel. The liquid it contains is of a soft rose-colour: the moment it begins to change its hue, awaken me – till then I may close my eyes. First, it will turn white, and then emit golden flashes; but wait not till then; when the rose-colour fades, rouse me.' I scarcely heard the last words, muttered, as they were, in sleep. Even then he did not quite yield to nature. 'Winzy, my boy,' he again said, 'do not touch the vessel – do not put it to your lips; it is a philter – a philter to cure love; you would not cease to love your Bertha – beware to drink!'

And he slept. His venerable head sunk on his breast, and I scarce heard his regular breathing. For a few minutes I watched the vessel – the rosy hue of the liquid remained unchanged. Then my thoughts wandered – they visited the fountain, and dwelt on a thousand charming scenes never to be renewed – never! Serpents and adders were in my heart as the word 'Never!' half formed itself on my lips. False girl! – false and cruel! Never more would she smile on me as that evening she smiled on Albert. Worthless, detested woman! I would not remain unrevenged – she should see Albert expire at her feet – she should die beneath my vengeance. She had smiled in disdain and triumph – she knew my wretchedness and her power. Yet what power had she? – the power of exciting my hate – my utter scorn – my – oh, all but indifference! Could I attain that – could I regard her with careless eyes, transferring my rejected love to one fairer and more true, that were indeed a victory!

A bright flash darted before my eyes. I had forgotten the medicine of the adept; I gazed on it with wonder: flashes of admirable beauty, more bright than those which the diamond emits when the sun's rays are on it, glanced from the surface of the liquid; an odour the most fragrant and grateful stole over my sense; the vessel seemed one globe of living radiance, lovely to the eye, and most inviting to the taste. The first thought, instinctively inspired by the grosser sense, was, I will – I must drink. I raised the vessel to my lips. 'It will cure me of love – of torture!' Already I had quaffed half of the most delicious liquor ever tasted by the palate of man, when the philosopher stirred. I started – I dropped the glass – the fluid flamed and glanced along the floor, while I felt Cornelius's gripe at my throat, as he shrieked aloud, 'Wretch! you have destroyed the labour of my life!'

The philosopher was totally unaware that I had drunk any portion of his drug. His idea was, and I gave a tacit assent to it, that I had raised the vessel from curiosity, and that, frighted at its brightness, and the flashes of intense light it gave forth, I had let it fall. I never undeceived him. The fire of the medicine was quenched – the fragrance died away – he grew calm, as a philosopher should under the heaviest trials, and dismissed me to rest.

I will not attempt to describe the sleep of glory and bliss which bathed my soul in paradise during the remaining hours of that memorable night. Words would be faint and shallow types of my enjoyment, or of the gladness that possessed my bosom when I woke. I trod air – my thoughts were in heaven. Earth appeared heaven, and my inheritance upon it was to be one trance of delight. 'This it is to be cured of love,' I thought; 'I will see Bertha this day, and she will find her lover cold and regardless; too happy to be disdainful, yet how utterly indifferent to her!'

The hours danced away. The philosopher, secure that he had once succeeded, and believing that he might again, began to concoct the same medicine once more. He was shut up with his books and drugs, and I had a holiday. I dressed myself with care; I looked in an old but polished shield, which served me for a mirror; methought my good looks had wonderfully improved. I hurried beyond the precincts of the town, joy in my soul, the beauty of heaven and earth around me. I turned my steps towards the castle – I could look on its lofty turrets with lightness of heart, for I was cured of love. My Bertha saw me afar off, as I came up the avenue. I know not what sudden impulse animated her bosom, but at the sight, she sprung with a light fawn-like bound down the marble steps, and was hastening towards me. But I had been perceived by another person. The old high-born hag, who called herself her protectress, and was her tyrant, had seen me also; she hobbled, panting, up the terrace; a page, as ugly as herself, held up her train, and fanned her as she hurried along, and stopped my fair girl with a 'How, now, my bold mistress? whither so fast? Back to your cage – hawks are abroad!'

Bertha clasped her hands – her eyes were still bent on my approaching figure. I saw the contest. How I abhorred the old crone who checked the kind impulses of my Bertha's softening heart. Hitherto, respect for her rank had caused me to avoid the lady of the castle; now I disdained such trivial considerations. I was cured of love, and lifted above all human fears; I hastened forwards, and soon reached the terrace. How lovely Bertha looked! Her eyes flashing fire, her cheeks glowing with impatience and anger, she was a thousand times more graceful and charming than ever. I no longer loved – Oh no! I adored – worshipped – idolised her!

She had that morning been persecuted, with more than usual vehemence, to consent to an immediate marriage with my rival. She was reproached with the encouragement that she had shown him – she was threatened with being turned out of doors with disgrace and shame. Her proud spirit rose in arms at the threat; but when she remembered the scorn that she had heaped upon me, and how, perhaps, she had thus lost one whom she now regarded as her only friend, she wept with remorse and rage. At that moment I appeared. 'Oh, Winzy!' she exclaimed, 'take me to your mother's cot; swiftly let me leave the detested luxuries and wretchedness of this noble dwelling – take me to poverty and happiness.'

I clasped her in my arms with transport. The old dame was speechless with fury, and broke forth into invective only when we were far on our road to my natal cottage. My mother received the fair fugitive, escaped from a gilt cage to nature and liberty, with tenderness and joy; my father, who loved her, welcomed her heartily; it was a day of rejoicing, which did not need the addition of the celestial potion of the alchymist to steep me in delight.

Soon after this eventful day, I became the husband of Bertha. I ceased to be the scholar of Cornelius, but I continued his friend. I always felt grateful to him for having, unawares, procured me that delicious draught of a divine elixir, which, instead of curing me of love (sad cure! solitary and joyless remedy for evils which seem blessings to the memory), had inspired me with courage and resolution, thus winning for me an inestimable treasure in my Bertha.

I often called to mind that period of trance-like inebriation with wonder. The drink of Cornelius had not fulfilled the task for which he affirmed that it had been prepared, but its effects were more potent and blissful than words can express. They had faded by degrees, yet they lingered long – and painted life in hues of splendour. Bertha often wondered at my lightness of heart and unaccustomed gaiety; for, before, I had been rather serious, or even sad, in my disposition. She loved me the better for my cheerful temper, and our days were winged by joy.

Five years afterwards I was suddenly summoned to the bedside of the dying Cornelius. He had sent for me in haste, conjuring my instant presence. I found him stretched on his pallet, enfeebled even to death; all of life that yet remained animated his piercing eyes, and they were fixed on a glass vessel, full of a roseate liquid.

'Behold,' he said, in a broken and inward voice, 'the vanity of human wishes! A second time my hopes are about to be crowned, a second time they are destroyed. Look at that liquor – you remember five years ago I had prepared the same, with the same success; – then, as now, my thirsting lips expected to taste the immortal elixir – you dashed it from me! and at present it is too late.'

He spoke with difficulty, and fell back on his pillow. I could not help saying –

'How, revered master, can a cure for love restore you to life?'

A faint smile gleamed across his face as I listened earnestly to his scarcely intelligible answer.

'A cure for love and for all things – the Elixir of Immortality. Ah! if now I might drink, I should live for ever!'

As he spoke, a golden flash gleamed from the fluid; a well-remembered fragrance stole over the air; he raised himself, all weak as he was – strength seemed miraculously to re-enter his frame – he stretched forth his hand – a loud explosion startled me – a ray of fire shot up from the elixir, and the glass vessel which contained it was shivered to atoms! I turned my eyes towards the philosopher; he had fallen back – his eyes were glassy – his features rigid – he was dead!

But I lived, and was to live for ever! So said the unfortunate alchymist, and for a few days I believed his words. I remembered the glorious intoxication that had followed my stolen draught. I reflected on the change I had felt in my frame – in my soul. The bounding elasticity of the one – the buoyant lightness of the other. I surveyed myself in a mirror, and could perceive no change in my features during the space of the five years which had elapsed. I remembered the radiant hues and grateful scent of that delicious beverage – worthy the gift it was capable of bestowing – I was, then, IMMORTAL!

A few days after I laughed at my credulity. The old proverb, that 'a prophet is least regarded in his own country,' was true with respect to me and my defunct master. I loved him as a man – I respected him as a sage – but I derided the notion that he could command the powers of darkness, and laughed at the superstitious fears with which he was regarded by the vulgar. He was a wise philosopher, but had no acquaintance with any spirits but those clad in flesh and blood. His science was simply human; and human science, I soon persuaded myself, could never conquer nature's laws so far as to imprison the soul for ever within its carnal habitation. Cornelius had brewed a soul-refreshing drink – more inebriating than wine – sweeter and more fragrant than any fruit: it possessed probably strong medicinal powers, imparting gladness to the heart and vigour to the limbs; but its effects would wear out; already were they diminished in my frame. I was a lucky fellow to have quaffed health and joyous spirits, and perhaps long life, at my master's hands; but my good fortune ended there: longevity was far different from immortality. I continued to entertain this belief for many years. Sometimes a thought stole across me – Was the alchymist indeed deceived? But my habitual credence was, that I should meet the fate of all the children of Adam at my appointed time – a little late, but still at a natural age. Yet it was certain that I retained a wonderfully youthful look. I was laughed at for my vanity in consulting the mirror so often, but I consulted it in vain – my brow was untrenched – my cheeks – my eyes – my whole person continued as untarnished as in my twentieth year.

I was troubled. I looked at the faded beauty of Bertha – I seemed more like her son. By degrees our neighbours began to make similar observations, and I found at last that I went by the name of the Scholar bewitched. Bertha herself grew uneasy. She became jealous and peevish, and at length she began to question me. We had no children; we were all in all to each other; and though, as she grew older, her vivacious spirit became a little allied to ill-temper, and her beauty sadly diminished, I cherished her in my heart as the mistress I had idolised, the wife I had sought and won with such perfect love.

At last our situation became intolerable: Bertha was fifty – I twenty years of age. I had, in very shame, in some measure adopted the habits of a more advanced age; I no longer mingled in the dance among the young and gay, but my heart bounded along with them while I restrained my feet; and a sorry figure I cut among the Nestors of our village. But before the time I mention, things were altered – we were universally shunned; we were – at least, I was – reported to have kept up an iniquitous acquaintance with some of my former master's supposed friends. Poor Bertha was pitied, but deserted. I was regarded with horror and detestation.

What was to be done? We sat by our winter fire – poverty had made itself felt, for none would buy the produce of my farm; and often I had been forced to journey twenty miles, to some place where I was not known, to dispose of our property. It is true, we had saved something for an evil day – that day was come.

We sat by our lone fireside – the old-hearted youth and his antiquated wife. Again Bertha insisted on knowing the truth; she recapitulated all she had ever heard said about me, and added her own observations. She conjured me to cast off the spell; she described how much more comely grey hairs were than my chestnut locks; she descanted on the reverence and respect due to age – how preferable to the slight regard paid to mere children: could I imagine that the despicable gifts of youth and good looks outweighed disgrace, hatred, and scorn? Nay, in the end I should be burnt as a dealer in the black art, while she, to whom I had not deigned to communicate any portion of my good fortune, might be stoned as my accomplice. At length she insinuated that I must share my secret with her, and bestow on her like benefits to those I myself enjoyed, or she would denounce me – and then she burst into tears.

Thus beset, methought it was the best way to tell the truth. I revealed it as tenderly as I could, and spoke only of a very long life, not of immortality – which representation, indeed, coincided best with my own ideas. When I ended, I rose and said, –

'And now, my Bertha, will you denounce the lover of your youth? – You will not, I know. But it is too hard, my poor wife, that you should suffer from my ill-luck and the accursed arts of

Cornelius. I will leave you – you have wealth enough, and friends will return in my absence. I will go; young as I seem, and strong as I am, I can work and gain my bread among strangers, unsuspected and unknown. I loved you in youth; God is my witness that I would not desert you in age, but that your safety and happiness require it.'

I took my cap and moved towards the door; in a moment Bertha's arms were round my neck, and her lips were pressed to mine. 'No, my husband, my Winzy,' she said, 'you shall not go alone – take me with you; we will remove from this place, and, as you say, among strangers we shall be unsuspected and safe. I am not so very old as quite to shame you, my Winzy; and I daresay the charm will soon wear off, and, with the blessing of God, you will become more elderly-looking, as is fitting; you shall not leave me.'

I returned the good soul's embrace heartily. 'I will not, my Bertha; but for your sake I had not thought of such a thing. I will be your true, faithful husband while you are spared to me, and do my duty by you to the last.'

The next day we prepared secretly for our emigration. We were obliged to make great pecuniary sacrifices – it could not be helped. We realised a sum sufficient, at least, to maintain us while Bertha lived; and, without saying adieu to any one, quitted our native country to take refuge in a remote part of western France.

It was a cruel thing to transport poor Bertha from her native village, and the friends of her youth, to a new country, new language, new customs. The strange secret of my destiny rendered this removal immaterial to me; but I compassionated her deeply, and was glad to perceive that she found compensation for her misfortunes in a variety of little ridiculous circumstances. Away from all tell-tale chroniclers, she sought to decrease the apparent disparity of our ages by a thousand feminine arts – rouge, youthful dress, and assumed juvenility of manner. I could not be angry. Did not I myself wear a mask? Why quarrel with hers, because it was less successful? I grieved deeply when I remembered that this was my Bertha, whom I had loved so fondly, and won with such transport – the dark-eyed, dark-haired girl, with smiles of enchanting archness and a step like a fawn – this mincing, simpering, jealous old woman. I should have revered her grey locks and withered cheeks; but thus! – It was my work, I knew; but I did not the less deplore this type of human weakness.

Her jealousy never slept. Her chief occupation was to discover that, in spite of outward appearances, I was myself growing old. I verily believe that the poor soul loved me truly in her heart, but never had woman so tormenting a mode of displaying fondness. She would discern wrinkles in my face and decrepitude in my walk, while I bounded along in youthful vigour, the youngest looking of twenty youths. I never dared address another woman. On one occasion, fancying that the belle of the village regarded me with favouring eyes, she brought me a grey wig. Her constant discourse among her acquaintances was, that though I looked so young, there was ruin at work within my frame; and she affirmed that the worst symptom about me was my apparent health. My youth was a disease, she said, and I ought at all times to prepare, if not for a sudden and awful death, at least to awake some morning white-headed and bowed down with all the marks of advanced years. I let her talk – I often joined in her conjectures. Her warnings chimed in with my never-ceasing speculations concerning my state, and I took an earnest, though painful, interest in listening to all that her quick wit and excited imagination could say on the subject.

Why dwell on these minute circumstances? We lived on for many long years. Bertha became bedrid and paralytic; I nursed her as a mother might a child. She grew peevish, and still harped upon one string – of how long I should survive her. It has ever been a source of consolation to me, that I performed my duty scrupulously towards her. She had been mine in youth, she was mine in age; and at last, when I heaped the sod over her corpse, I wept to feel that I had lost all that really bound me to humanity.

Since then how many have been my cares and woes, how few and empty my enjoyments! I pause here in my history – I will pursue it no further. A sailor without rudder or compass, tossed on a stormy sea – a traveller lost on a widespread heath, without landmark or stone to guide him – such have I been: more lost, more hopeless than either. A nearing ship, a gleam from some far cot, may save them; but I have no beacon except the hope of death.

Death! Mysterious, ill-visaged friend of weak humanity! Why alone of all mortals have you cast me from your sheltering fold? Oh, for the peace of the grave! The deep silence of the iron-bound tomb! That thought would cease to work in my brain, and my heart beat no more with emotions varied only by new forms of sadness!

Am I immortal? I return to my first question. In the first place, is it not more probable that the beverage of the alchymist was fraught rather with longevity than eternal life? Such is my hope. And then be it remembered, that I only drank half of the potion prepared by him. Was not the whole necessary to complete the charm? To have drained half the Elixir of Immortality is but to be half-immortal – my For-ever is thus truncated and null.

But again, who shall number the years of the half of eternity? I often try to imagine by what rule the infinite may be divided. Sometimes I fancy age advancing upon me. One grey hair I have found. Fool! Do I lament? Yes, the fear of age and death often creeps coldly into my heart; and the more I live, the more I dread death, even while I abhor life. Such an enigma is man – born to perish – when he wars, as I do, against the established laws of his nature. But for this anomaly of feeling surely I might die: the medicine of the alchymist would not be proof against fire – sword – and the strangling waters. I have gazed upon the blue depths of many a placid lake, and the tumultuous rushing of many a mighty river, and have said, peace inhabits those waters; yet I have turned my steps away, to live yet another day. I have asked myself, whether suicide would be a crime in one to whom thus only the portals of the other world could be opened. I have done all, except presenting myself as a soldier or duellist, an object of destruction to my – no, not my fellow-mortals, and therefore I have shrunk away. They are not my fellows. The inextinguishable power of life in my frame, and their ephemeral existence, places us wide as the poles asunder. I could not raise a hand against the meanest or the most powerful among them.

Thus I have lived on for many a year – alone, and weary of myself – desirous of death, yet never dying – a mortal immortal. Neither ambition nor avarice can enter my mind, and the ardent love that gnaws at my heart, never to be returned – never to find an equal on which to expend itself – lives there only to torment me.

This very day I conceived a design by which I may end all – without self-slaughter, without making another man a Cain – an expedition, which mortal frame can never survive, even endued with the youth and strength that inhabits mine. Thus I shall put my immortality to the test, and rest for ever – or return, the wonder and benefactor of the human species.

Before I go, a miserable vanity has caused me to pen these pages. I would not die, and leave no name behind. Three centuries have passed since I quaffed the fatal beverage; another year shall not elapse before, encountering gigantic dangers – warring with the powers of frost in their home – beset by famine, toil, and tempest – I yield this body, too tenacious a cage for a soul which thirsts for freedom, to the destructive elements of air and water; or, if I survive, my name shall be recorded as one of the most famous among the sons of men; and, my task achieved, I shall adopt more resolute means, and, by scattering and annihilating the atoms that compose my frame, set at liberty the life imprisoned within, and so cruelly prevented from soaring from this dim earth to a sphere more congenial to its immortal essence.

Mary Shelley's Reading List in Bath

List of books read in 1816

(Those marked * [Percy] Shelley has read also.)

4 vols. of Clarendon's *History* [*of the Rebellion and Civil Wars in England*, 3 vols, 1702–1704]

* *Bertram* [by Charles R. Maturin, 1816]

Vancenza. By Mrs [Mary] Robinson [2 vols, 1792]

Antiquary [by Sir Walter Scott, 3 vols, Edinburgh, 1816]

* *Edinburgh Review*. No. LII. [June 1816, vol. 26]

Chrononhotonthologus [by Henry Carey, 1734]

* *Fazio* [by Henry H. Milman, 1815]

Love and Madness [by Sir Herbert Croft, 1780]

Memoirs of Princess of Bareith [by Frederica Sophia Wilhelmina of Prussia, Consort of Frederick William, Margrave of Brandenburg-Bayreuth]

* Letters of *Emile* [by Jean-Jacques Rousseau, 1762]

The latter part of *Clarissa Harlowe* [*Clarissa* by Samuel Richardson, 7 vols, 1748]

Clarendon's *History of the Civil War* [a repetition]

* *Life of Holcroft* [by Holcroft himself, completed by
	William Hazlitt, 3 vols, 1816]
* *Glenarvon* [by Lady Caroline Lamb, 1816]
Patronage [by Maria Edgeworth, 4 vols, 1814]
The Milesian Chief [by Charles R. Maturin, 4 vols, 1812]
O'Donnel [by Lady Morgan, 3 vols, 1814]
* *Don Quixote* [by Miguel de Cervantes, 1605]
* Vita Alexandri Quintii Curtii
Conspiration de Rienzi [by Joseph François Laignelot, 1790]
Introduction to Davy's Chemistry [*Elements of Chemical
	Philosophy*, 1812]
Les Incas [Jean Françoise Marmontel, 1777]
Bryan Perdue [*Memoirs of Bryan Perdue* by Thomas Holcroft,
	3 vols, 1805]
Sir C. Grandison [*The History of Sir Charles Grandison* by
	Samuel Richardson, 7 vols, 1754]
Castle Rackrent [by Maria Edgeworth, 1800]
Gulliver's Travels [by Jonathan Swift, 1726]
Paradise Lost [by John Milton, 1667]
* *Pamela* [by Samuel Richardson, 2 vols, 1741]
* 3 vols. of Gibbon [*Decline and Fall of the Roman Empire*,
	12 vols, 1783-90]
1 book of Locke's Essay [*Concerning Human Understanding*, 1690]
Some of Horace's Odes
*Edinburgh Review, LIII [September 1816, Vol. 27]
Rights of Women [*A Vindication of the Rights of Woman*
	by Mary Wollstonecraft, 1792]

'De Senectute' by Cicero

2 vols of Lord Chesterfield's *Letters to his Son* [2 vols, 1774]

* *Story of Rimini* [by Leigh Hunt, 1816]

List of books read in 1817

2 vols of Lord Chesterfield's *Letters* [2 vols, 1774]

* Coleridge's *Lay Sermon* [1817]

Memoirs of Count Grammont [by Anthony Hamilton, 1714]

Somnium Scipionis [by Cicero]

Roderick Random [*The Adventures of Roderick Random* by Tobias Smollett, 2 vols, 1748]

Comus [by John Milton, 1637]

Knights of the Swan [by Madame de Genlis; translated by Rev. Beresford, 3 vols, 1796]

[Richard] Cumberland's *Memoirs* [2 parts, 1806-07]

Junius's Letters [2 vols, 1772]

Cupid's Revenge [by Beaumont and Fletcher, 1612]

Martial [*Love's Cure, or the Martial Maid* by Beaumont and Fletcher, 1647]

Wild Goose [*The Wild Goose Chase* by Beaumont and Fletcher, 1621]

* *Tales of my Landlord* [by Sir Walter Scott, 1816]

Rambler [by Samuel Johnson, 1750-52]

* *Waverley* [by Sir Walter Scott, 1814]

Amadis de Gaul [*Amadis de Gaula* by Vasco de Lobeida, *c.*1508; translated by Robert Southey]

Suggested Further Reading

Primary Works

Mary Shelley, *Frankenstein; or, The Modern Prometheus* (London: Lackington), 1818

Mary Shelley, *Tales and Stories*, introduced by Richard Garnett (London: William Paterson & Co.), 1891

Letters and Journals

Betty T. Bennett (ed.), *The Letters of Mary Wollstonecraft Shelley*, 3 vols (Baltimore and London: John Hopkins University Press), 1980–88

Paula R. Feldman and Diana Scott-Kilvert (eds), *Mary Shelley, Journals*, 2 vols (Oxford: Oxford University Press), 1987

Frederick L. Jones (ed.), *Mary Shelley's Journal* (Norman: University of Oklahoma Press), 1947

Secondary Materials

Charlotte Gordon, *Romantic Outlaws: The Extraordinary Lives of Mary Wollstonecraft and Mary Shelley* (London: Penguin, 2015)

Daisy Hay, *Young Romantics* (London: Bloomsbury), 2010

Anne K. Mellor, *Mary Shelley: Her Life, Her Fiction, Her Monsters* (New York: Routledge), 1988

Fiona Sampson, *In Search of Mary Shelley: The Girl Who Wrote Frankenstein* (London: Profile Books), 2028

Miranda Seymour, *Mary Shelley* (London: John Murray), 2000

Muriel Spark, *Child of Light (Child of Light: A Reassessment of Mary Wollstonecraft Shelley)* (Essex: Tower Bridge Publications Limited), 1951. Revised edition: *Mary Shelley* (London: Constable), 1988

Emily W. Sunstein, *Mary Shelley: Romance and Reality* (New York: Little, Brown and Co.), 1989

CONTRIBUTORS

Mary Shelley (1797–1851) was an English novelist best known for her groundbreaking work *Frankenstein; or, The Modern Prometheus* (1818), which is considered one of the earliest examples of science fiction. Born Mary Wollstonecraft Godwin, she was the daughter of the philosopher William Godwin and the pioneering feminist writer Mary Wollstonecraft. Tragically, her mother died shortly after her birth, and Mary was raised by her father in an intellectually stimulating environment. In 1814, Mary began a relationship with the poet Percy Bysshe Shelley, and the couple eloped to Europe. Their relationship was marked by scandal, as Shelley was already married, but it also fostered a rich creative partnership. The idea for *Frankenstein* came to Mary Godwin during a summer sojourn in 1816 with Percy Shelley on the shores of Lake Geneva, where Lord Byron was also staying. She was inspired to begin her unique tale after Byron suggested a ghost story competition. Byron himself produced 'A Fragment,' which later inspired his physician John Polidori to write *The Vampyre*. Mary completed her short story back in England, Chapter 4 of which was written during her stay in Bath. Among her other novels are *The Last Man* (1826), a dystopian story set in the twenty-first century, *The Fortunes of Perkin Warbeck* (1830), *Lodore* (1835) and *Falkner* (1837). As well as contributing many stories and essays to publications such as the *Keepsake* and the *Westminster Review*, she wrote numerous biographical essays for Lardner's *Cabinet Cyclopaedia*. Her other books include the first collected edition of Percy Bysshe Shelley's *Poetical Works* (1839) and a book based on the Continental travels she undertook with her son Percy Florence and his friends, *Rambles in Germany and Italy* (1844)

Professor Fiona Sampson MBE FRSL is a highly regarded British poet, writer and critic, known for her significant contributions to contemporary literature. Born in London in 1963, Sampson has published numerous poetry collections, including *The Distance Between Us*, *Coleshill* and *The Catch*, which showcase her refined, lyrical style and deep exploration of human experience. Her work often delves into themes of identity, nature and memory, marked by a careful attention to language and form. In addition to her poetry, Sampson has written extensively in other genres, including biography and criticism. One of her most acclaimed works is *In Search of Mary Shelley: The Girl Who Wrote Frankenstein*, a biography that offers a fresh perspective on the life and legacy of this iconic author. Sampson's contributions to literature have been recognised with numerous awards, and she has been shortlisted for prestigious honours such as the T.S. Eliot Prize. She has also been a significant figure in the literary community through her editorial work and her role as a professor of poetry at the University of Roehampton.

Eleanor Macnair is a British artist best known for her unique and imaginative project *Photographs Rendered in Play-Doh*. Her work involves recreating famous photographs using the colourful and malleable medium of Play-Doh, which she then photographs. The project began as a playful experiment but quickly gained international recognition for its innovative approach to reinterpreting iconic images. Macnair's work has been exhibited in galleries around the world, and she has published books featuring her Play-Doh recreations. Beyond this project, she is also active in the fields of photography and visual arts as a writer, editor and curator. Please visit her website: *eleanormacnair.com*

MANDERLEY PRESS TITLES

***Edinburgh: Picturesque Notes* by Robert Louis Stevenson**
Introduced by Alexander McCall Smith
Illustrated by Iain McIntosh

***The Armourer's House* by Rosemary Sutcliff**
Introduced by Lara Maiklem
Illustrated by Isabel Greenberg

***Appointment with Venus* by Jerrard Tickell**
Introduced by Rosa Rankin-Gee
Illustrated by Edward Bawden

***The Fly on the Wheel* by Katherine Cecil Thurston**
Introduced by Megan Nolan
Illustrated by Kathi Burke

***Letter from New York* by Helene Hanff**
Introduced by Jean Hanff Korelitz
Illustrated by Bruce Eric Kaplan

***China Court* by Rumer Godden**
Introduced by Linda Grant
Illustrated by Emily Maude

***The House in Cornwall* by Noel Streatfeild**
Introduced by Lucy Mangan
Illustrated by Elly Jahnz

***Tales of London Town* by Joan Aiken**
Introduced by Kiran Millwood Hargrave
Illustrated by Annabel Pearl

Florence: Ordeal by Water **by Kathrine Kressmann Taylor**
Introduced by Vanessa Nicolson
Illustrated by Agnesbic

Washington Square **by Henry James**
Introduced by Colm Tóibín
Illustrated by Rose Wong

Mary Shelley in Bath
Introduced by Fiona Sampson
Illustrated by Eleanor Macnair

Sun Horse, Moon Horse **by Rosemary Sutcliff**
Introduced by Tiffany Francis-Baker
Illustrated by Isabel Greenberg

The Strange House **by Raymond Briggs**
Introduced by Chris Riddell
Illustrated by Raymond Briggs